I0517895

Tattoos

&Pearls

Tattoos

&Pearls

Combining Street Wisdom
With Corporate Strategy

Miriam Simon

ROSALES MAVERICKS
PUBLISHING STUDIO

Copyright © 2025 Miriam Simon
Title: Tattoos and Pearls
Subtitle: Combining Street Wisdom with Corporate Strategy
Version 3nd

ISBN: 978-1-959471-59-2 (Paperback)
ISBN: 978-1-959471-79-0 (Hardback)
ISBN: 978-1-959471-60-8 (e-Book)

Library of Congress Control Number: 2025903711

Business | Women | Hispanic | LGBTQ+

Cover design by RMPStudio™ Team
Edited by: RMPStudio™ Team
Printed in the United States of America
Las Vegas Nevada 89144
From cover photography: Miram Simon and RMPStudio Team™

Publisher: RMPS, Rosales Mavericks Publishing Studio™,1180 N. Town Center Suite #100, Las Vegas, Nevada 89144, www.Adriana.Company

No part of this book may be reproduced, stored in a retrieval system, or transmitted in any form or by any means, electronic, mechanical, photocopying, recording, scanning, or otherwise, without the prior written permission of the author.

Limit of Liability/Disclaimer of Warranty:
The publisher and author have made every effort to ensure the accuracy and completeness of this book's contents. However, they do not guarantee that the contents are free from errors or omissions and disclaim any implied warranties of merchantability or fitness for a particular purpose. No warranty may be created or extended by sales representatives or written sales materials. The advice and strategies contained in this book may not be suitable for every situation. Professional consultation is recommended where appropriate. All events are loosely based on actual events and fictionalized characters. Advisory to Readers: This book contains descriptions of traumatic events, including childhood abuse, violence, death, and other potentially triggering content that some readers may find distressing. Reader discretion is advised.

The publisher and author shall not be responsible for any loss of profit or any other commercial damages, including but not limited to special, incidental, consequential, or other damages arising from the use of or inability to use this book.

"I.N.K. Your Story.
Wear Your Wisdom.
Lead for Generations."

-Miriam Simon

*For my greatest mentor, my chosen mom,
who planted the seed the moment
she met me to write a book!
And for my parents who
undoubtedly paid the ultimate
price for our happiness.*

Contents

MIRIAM SIMON

HONOR YOU

DEDICATION

This book is dedicated to all individuals who have felt invisible. We have lived quietly in the background and in the shadows. At times, we have been quiet in our chaos, in our fight, and in our wants and needs. We have constantly avoided our own voice by suppressing and silencing our longing to be heard. Due to necessity, perhaps, or because we have been busy catering to others' needs instead of our own. We have learned that invisibility helps us stay alive and live another day. For others, invisibility may have been the only way our parents would accept us. For some, invisibility has kept us safe from judgment and harm. Invisibility may have also kept us comfortable in new circumstances. We may not even know we are living in invisibility, yet it has scarred most of us at some point in our lives.

Regardless of the reason for being invisible (knowingly or unknowingly), the day will come when you can take no more, when someone has taken it too far. They have gone beyond our threshold, but, perhaps, we may have allowed it. When you find that your voice has value, has impact, and has the ability to keep you safe and to thrive in life, we have no other option but to become visible. There comes a moment when the deepest part of you is ready to burst open because the pain is so intolerable. That part of you is waiting to burst deep from within the heart. It is a scary moment, but one choice can help you move forward. There will be some unlearning that will happen, but eventually, you emerge in your wholeness and shine brightly.

This book is dedicated to the person who passed away saving my life in a drive-by shooting when I was 17 years old. Although our time together was short, he has been worth countless lives. And so I say:

"Dear Juan, I've been able to touch countless lives in your absence. I learned pure joy from your friendship during our walks together to Pulaski Park. You brought a smile to my face every time we waved hello to each other from my 4-story building window to yours, every time you dialed 778-2215, my grandparents' landline. Our time together was pure fun, thanks to every joke you made. Our laughs were heard loud and clear, far and near. I thank you for taking the beer cans out of my hands and letting me know I was worthy of more than my current circumstances and environment. The trust we shared allowed me to know that I could trust the love I later found in life. I found my wife, who means the world to me, today, who, by the way, continues to love, honor, and support me because I knew love from you.

Since your physical departure, I've known you've been with me. I feel the same chilling sensation on my right arm tattoo after you playfully bit it. I remember when you shared with me that we were about to part ways because you thought you were going away to jail. Little did we know that was your goodbye message to me for life. The next few months were a complete black hole for me, filled with desperation, confusion, and loneliness because everything & everyone we knew changed the day you passed away. I did find true love eventually, like you wished for me, and I appreciate you taking a step back in your afterlife so I could be with her.
Because you saved my life, I live unapologetically."

𝕸𝖎𝖗𝖎𝖆𝖒 𝕾𝖎𝖒𝖔𝖓, jefa de jefas

3

FOREWORD

The first time I shook Miriam Simon's hand at the LinkedIn LeanIn Latinas leadership conference in 2024, I felt something rare, that unmistakable electricity when you meet someone whose journey mirrors parts of your own, yet blazes trails you've yet to walk. Among hundreds of accomplished Latina professionals, Miriam wasn't just present; she was fully immersed, asking questions that made speakers pause and reflect, and connecting with everyone in a way that made them feel truly seen.

As a woman who traveled my own path from humble beginnings to professional success, I recognized in Miriam a kindred spirit who understood that our backgrounds aren't burdens to overcome, but rather rich soil from which our greatest strengths grow. Her story resonated deeply with me because, like many of us who've crossed borders both literally and figuratively, Miriam refused to leave her authentic self behind as she ascended the corporate ladder.

What makes **"Tattoos and Pearls"** extraordinary and what moved me personally is how Miriam transforms her journey from a one-bedroom apartment in Passaic, NJ, to executive leadership into universal wisdom accessible to all of us. Reading her manuscript, I found myself nodding, sometimes laughing, occasionally wiping away tears, and repeatedly thinking, "I wish I'd had this book twenty years ago."

This isn't just another success story. It's an intimate blueprint for those of us who've ever felt we needed to choose between our cultural identity, staying invisible, and our professional ambitions. Miriam's candid accounts of navigating corporate spaces while honoring her Mexican heritage reminded me of my own struggles and triumphs, validating experiences I rarely see reflected in leadership literature.

The timing of this book couldn't be more perfect. As organizations finally begin to recognize that authentic leadership and diverse perspectives aren't just nice-to-haves but competitive advantages, Miriam offers practical guidance on leveraging employee resource groups, building meaningful networks, and maintaining integrity while advancing in the corporate ladder.

"Tattoos and Pearls" has already changed how I approach my own leadership journey. I believe it will have the same effect on you. Miriam's story reminds us all that leadership isn't about fitting into predetermined molds; it's about breaking them open to create space for new possibilities and bringing others along with you.

This book is a gift. Treasure it.

Martha Niño, Author of "The Other Side:
From a Shack to Silicon Valley" and TEDx Speaker

HOW TO READ THIS BOOK

This is not your typical business or self-help book. This is raw, unfiltered wisdom earned through blood, sweat, and survival. To get the most from these pages, I invite you to approach them with both your heart and your strategic mind open.

Start Where You Are

Whether you're a C-suite executive with "tattoos" hidden beneath your suit or someone fighting your way up from rock bottom, this book meets you exactly where you are. There's no prerequisite for transformation except honesty with yourself.

Engage with the Framework

Throughout these chapters, you'll encounter two powerful frameworks:

The I.N.K. Framework will help you honor your battle-tested instinct, create strategic navigation maps, and develop a killer mindset that refuses to back down.

The P.E.A.R.L.S. Strategy guides you through Positioning, Executing, Adapting, Resilience, leveraging resources, and claiming your Sovereignty.

Take Action

Each chapter ends with specific action steps designed to move you from insight to implementation. Don't just read them, do them. Real transformation happens in the application.

Use the Companion Resources

To deepen your experience:

- Complete **The Tattoos & Pearls Companion Workbook** to apply insights in your own context
- Take advantage of the **FREE 5-Step Quick Start Guide** to begin aligning your experiences with leadership strategy
- Join the **90-Minute Live Pearls of Wisdom Webinar** for direct guidance on activating your leadership power

Read with Both Head and Heart

The stories shared here, from contemplating a life altering event as a child, to witnessing death up close to fighting for my children's lives, are not just emotional narratives. They contain strategic lessons about intuition, advocacy, and uncompromising determination that apply equally in the streets and the boardroom.

Recognize Your Own Wisdom

As you read about my experiences and the lessons they've taught me, take time to reflect on your own life's wisdom. What have your challenges taught you? Where have you been playing small? What power are you not yet claiming?

Remember: This Is Not Theory

Everything in these pages has been tested in the most extreme circumstances. When I talk about trusting your instincts, it's because mine saved my daughter's life. When I discuss resilience, it's because I've rebuilt from absolute zero. These aren't strategies developed in a business school; they were forged in moments where everything was on the line.

Your story matters. Your survival matters. And the wisdom you've earned through your own battles is precisely what will fuel your leadership and transform your life. Let's get started.

INTRODUCTION
Why Tattoos and Pearls?

At a little over four decades of life, I learned that invisibility no longer serves me. Like a pearl hidden within its shell, I had concealed my body, my lifestyle, my intelligence, and my voice so others could feel comfortable. I realized that when I was authentic, others found me intimidating and not easily understood because I challenged the status quo; I am far from traditional and the opposite of stereotypical characteristics. Additionally, I recognized that people couldn't see beyond preconceived marginalized concepts because of my humble beginnings. I was astounded by what I brought to the table: the conviction of my views, passions, and ability to cut through the despair, chaos, and distractions. The ease with which I can speak to anyone, attract happiness, live freely, and invite abundance has been a key indicator of my choices to create my life now, but that doesn't come without a heavy price. My family and I have paid for it.

I realized that to step into full abundance, I needed to let go of invisibility. Just as tattoos make permanent marks on our skin, I needed to make permanent changes in my life. I took the time to get my body back into shape because of suffering from health issues. During this challenging time and recovery, my wife found countless ways to love me unconditionally. I had held back on my own happiness to make our families and others feel comfortable. I also realized that I did not fully accept myself and my complete identity. I learned to embrace my unique perspective on life, wisdom, and strategies to

9

win at love, life, and professionally. Now, I am able to share where I started, what I have been through, and how, like me, you can win in your personal and professional lives fearlessly. You too can own that you are worthy of all the happiness and joy life has to offer.

Throughout this journey, I developed two powerful frameworks that guided my transformation, I.N.K. and P.E.A.R.L.S., which I'll share with you throughout these pages. I.N.K. became my foundation: trusting my **Instinct** when others doubted me, learning to **Navigate** spaces not designed for people like me, and developing a **Killer mindset** that refused to accept limitations. This framework helped me survive when survival seemed impossible. (Yes, I'm an '80s baby, so you know what I mean when I say Killer Cool)

Many times in my life, I did not see my worth. I was operating from a place where people could see I wasn't giving 100%. Over the years, people at work, school, and in my personal life have asked for more from me. I always wondered what else I could give. What were they seeking from me? I already gave all I could give; I couldn't give any more. It wasn't until later in life that I understood what they kept asking.

I learned I was living in the shadows where I felt comfortable. Like a pearl still forming within its oyster shell, I emerged here and there, but I didn't stay consistent. I learned to retract my ability to feel safe. I placed one foot out, succeeded, and reverted to my safe space. Although my ambitious drive for achievement and service is unparalleled, a deep force continued to hold me back, which kept me inching forward day after day, but at the same time, in the same place - INVISIBILITY.

The fight with invisibility stems from my childhood, which has many highs and lows. I would thrive in one area and be undervalued in another. My voice was good enough in some spaces and then dismissed in others. My mind, body, and soul kept me alive and brought me opportunities, a thirst and curiosity for life, but I was taken advantage of. My innocence, kind-heartedness, and joy brought me fulfillment but were, in different ways, met with deception, betrayal, and cold-heartedness. Achievements that have taken me to unknown territory have also brought great envy, hurtful criticisms, and raised doubt within. These challenges were painful in various ways but simultaneously provided me with the pearls of wisdom to find a new way of life, break toxic cycles for myself and others, and bring happiness, fulfillment, and peace into my life.

This is where my P.E.A.R.L.S. strategy emerged from the polished approach that helped me move beyond survival to truly thrive. I learned the power of strategic **Positioning**, flawless **Execution**, nimble **Adaptability**, unwavering **Resilience** (with proper **Rewards**), intentional **Leverage**, and ultimate **Sovereignty**. Like actual pearls formed over time, this strategy took time to develop but has become my most valuable asset.

The various powers of high-tension strings propelled me up but pulled me down simultaneously, like a Cirque du Soleil acrobat. They were the foundational roots that sparked the tenacity to simply go for living life fully. The continuous tumultuous tension and fast-moving world marked me for life but gave me the power, tenacity, and

11

momentum to face fear. I also changed what wasn't working, created the life of my choice, continue to reach new peaks, and look back to give my hand and bring others with me.

Because I am no longer invisible, this is my invitation for you to feel the cool breeze in your hair on a flight with me and own your transformative journey. Like tattoos that tell a story on our skin, there is always an opposing theme that emerges from challenges, traumas, and perspectives. I am a better mother, partner, and grandmother. I am a better person overall because of the pearls of wisdom I have gained from all my past experiences. Admitting the truth is hard, but I know that it will help and guide someone. The truth will help you see the depression and deception that may still at times linger without you knowing. It will make clear the thoughts of inability, immobilization, loneliness, and instability. And when things are clear, these things will fade away because now you can identify them, and this makes all the difference in the world.

In this book, I want to reveal how life often differs from its outward appearance. Many people face hidden struggles, navigating through difficult circumstances and enduring hardships that may not be visible to others. For some, challenging days outnumber the good ones, creating a reality that few understand. By sharing my journey with you, my hope is that you, the reader, can understand that regardless of what you're going through, you're going to be OK as long as you work towards doing good deeds and being a good person. I know they say the nice girl doesn't get the corner office and things like that, but I beg to differ. There hasn't been a moment that I regretted being a good or nice person, and those who cannot honor me do not belong within my circle of influence.

Like a pearl slowly forming around an irritant, life's hardest days often teach us the most valuable lessons. You'll encounter people with harmful intentions who may show little patience for your journey. In a world filled with negativity, you might feel neglected, discarded, or worthless at times. I've experienced all these struggles and more. When I reached adulthood, I immediately began working on myself, determined to leave those painful experiences behind. This journey of self-improvement has shown me that growth is a continuous process. Regardless of our age, we all benefit from continuing our personal development to move forward in life.

I am putting my life to ink and paper because it is important for me to share my stories of neglect, deceit, and chaos to give people hope and strength, embrace their individuality, and have faith that everything is temporary and sometimes even an illusion. To also reiterate that doing the work truly helps! Reading enriches your journey. Developing self-awareness serves you well. Recognizing toxicity in your life matters, if any exists. Becoming aware of the nonsense around you, the chaos, the mess, the people who don't support you, and those who only wish to use you, can truly transform your path. The same way there are negative people in various environments, there are others who see the good in you. These are the people who will help you, who support you, who will help you move forward. All in all, life is great and good, and our greatest asset will always be seeing both the good and the bad. In my line of work, I recognize what Tony Robbins would call distinctions. As you become more aware and more attuned to who you are, you will realize that making distinctions is important, but more important is staying true to yourself, the good part of yourself, the best part of yourself. This is what I want to convey in this book: the goodness in you and in all of us.

Throughout these chapters, you'll see how I.N.K. helped me survive my darkest moments and how P.E.A.R.L.S. elevated me to heights I never imagined possible. This is not just a framework, it's your roadmap from wherever you are to wherever you dare to dream of going.

Just like tattoos, experiences and moments shift and change who you are and sometimes mark you for life. Regardless of what you go through in life, recognizing your inner wisdom is crucial. I may have, in the past, seemed like a rough and tough person, protecting myself due to my life experiences, but with it all, the wisdom I gained from Tattoos and Pearls in my life journey was worth every experience. I hope that you see the pearls and marvel at the tattoos.

FRACTURED FOUNDATIONS
From Red Bricks to Black Ink

Maslow's hierarchy of needs became a revelation when I was introduced to the concept through Unleash the Power Within with Tony Robbins at the age of 23. An **AHA** moment struck, and the world stopped. Life appeared to be all wrong! No wonder self-actualization remained out of my reach - that phase in life where your wildest dreams unfold, guided by the foresight to envision the future and the strategies to accomplish your goals. Four fundamental human needs: physiological, safety, belonging, and healthy self-esteem had been missing throughout my childhood. Adulthood provided the first real opportunity to obtain these fundamentals, mainly through personal effort. When resources or knowledge were lacking, seeking help from others became necessary to level up. The impact of these unmet needs, invisible to many, shaped everything for me. Deliberate work on reaching each of these needs made my present life possible. What I'm about to share with you may astonish you, but trust me, it all happened, and I'm still here, striving and still learning.

Success for me in the professional realm required an inward journey first. My growth remained ongoing; now the story is ready to be shared. The invisible aspects of my life, the ones embedded in my mind, body, and spirit, must be acknowledged, and through this book, I do exactly that. Habits, thoughts, and circumstances, formed by those souls who influenced my personal development, created patterns that shaped my existence. Awareness of these influences allowed me to audit both my internal and external processes: recalibrating and reducing them to ashes. A new version emerged when the old me dissolved into the atmosphere. Countless powers guided me and my existence on this earth. Personal experiences, familiar to many in varying degrees of intensity, will be shared. In this chapter I share the good, the bad and the ugly because you must have the ability to distinguish between them all.

In my life journey I started at negative zero with a foundation that was short of being anything but the American dream. Growing up resembled a raw, cold reality where everything felt like red-brown brick buildings like the kind you see in the movies where chaos surfaces and the police never arrive because it's presumed that part of the city doesn't matter. Every word in this chapter could be written in red capital letters. The alarming sight of my neighborhood would make the average American cringe. A huge stop sign helping guide me to a much better way of living and seeing the world would have been so helpful back then. However, gratitude exists for my journey as it is uniquely mine and mine alone. As time progressed, I learned a thing or two about what it means to have an attitude of abundance. As I have been able to see both sides of one coin. Throughout my life, I had to create my own guiding rails since growing up I had none.

My Financial Reality Throughout the Years

In the past, while in my twenties and working in the corporate arena, one of my biggest red flags hindering my independence and impact on my financial health was learning the difference between poor and broke: poor is forever, broke is temporary. Living in survival mode instead of peace became the norm when money was scarce at home. This example is key to my point. In finance, being in the red signals a deficit, while Black Friday represents the moment profits begin because of the influx of money. Scarcity became my relentless twin, a presence that refused to leave, a shadow that made existence feel temporary and unstable due to the lack of finances. Every achievement felt fleeting as if everything I worked for could vanish in an instant because of my limiting beliefs at the time. As I recollect where I developed my belief systems, I've gained insight and re-educated my thought process as it pertains to finances.

A childhood marked by lack defined my reality. Not enough food. Not enough clothes. Not enough space. Not enough money. Not enough safety. Not enough self-worth. Scarcity pervaded my home, my school, and my community. The saying, "you can't buy happiness," fails to apply when basic needs remain unmet. An empty stomach, an aching body, a broken heart, and the looming threat of homelessness overshadowed any chance at peace. Streets were riddled with danger, which made survival the primary concern, with thoughts occupied by the possibility of life-altering or life-ending events. Yet here I am standing strong with a new way of knowing true wealth and financial freedom.

Being in survival mode all the time is an unsustainable way of living. When you live this way, you are dominated by fear, conflict, avoidance, hypervigilance, and despair. Love, aspirations, and hope existed in fragments but failed to outweigh the overarching theme of deprivation. Uncertainty and anger clouded my home, my school, and my neighborhood, making the future feel impossible to grasp. Yet again here I am an overcomer and seeing my true value. Each moment had to be lived as if it were the last. Happiness surfaced in glimpses, yet the glass remained empty, rarely even half full. When something was gained, it disappeared as quickly as it arrived, spread too thin among competing needs. As the oldest of seven, technically eight, because one of my sisters passed away before turning a month old. My family responsibilities and the noise around me were as complicated as my living situation. As the first granddaughter and cousin on my father's side, expectations loomed heavily. My mother's family remained in Mexico, with limited communication.

A particular memory from age 11 replays often in my head. For six years, it had just been my brother and I, then my first sister arrived. Then my second sister came. And then a third sister was on the way. Frustration and sadness surged not because I didn't love my sisters, but because we had no food to eat, no clothes to wear, no more space for one more person to sleep and we had nothing more to share. Why did my mother keep having babies? A question that lingered in my young mind, devoid of understanding. All I remember was my mother's deep happiness for a new child, that was to us, traditionally and religiously speaking, a gift from God, but we also knew we were struggling. At this point, scarcity was rampant. To add insult to injury, my father, an alcoholic, violent, and deeply disturbing man, fueled chaos. He didn't support us financially or emotionally. And still, the question I kept asking was why did my mother continue having children with him? I didn't get it. Throughout my entire life, the relationship with my father was nonexistent. "Dad" was never a word I used. His presence signified fights, yelling, and pain. Sometimes, his presence fueled imminent death if not navigated carefully. His selfishness knew no bounds, visiting only my mother while his children remained afterthoughts. In retrospect, even Bellamy, the Persian cat belonging to my daughter, received more interaction and acknowledgment than we did back then.

More Scarcity and Worker Exploitation

More children arriving in an already stretched-thin household felt incomprehensible. The one-bedroom apartment barely accommodated the existing family. Money for food remained scarce. My mother, working as a seamstress, earned just enough to cover rent, heat, and electricity. Factories often closed unexpectedly, leaving workers without jobs or paychecks, debts still remain unpaid to this day. These factories operated on exploitation, using women for labor, then vanishing without compensation. This exploitation extended beyond my mother to my grandmother, with women in the neighborhood joining together to demand their earnings, only to be ignored. The system failed them, leaving families in deeper financial distress. Government assistance filled gaps, yet feeding multiple mouths remained a challenge. Hard-working women with integrity and untapped talents deserved more, but circumstances locked them in cycles of survival.

Faces of despair became common within my view, mothers robbed of wages in my community, families denied financial stability was commonplace, many workers were dismissed without warning. All that was left at times was to go file for unemployment benefits until a new factory opened up in our town. These

19

women did not drive and each family that happened to own a vehicle would be driven by the father. Mostly all women walked to work and wanted to be close to home to care for their children before and after school. I recall walking with my mother and grandmother approximately 20 minutes to the local unemployment office. Walking uptown, doing whatever could be done, all while going without. We were already at a deficit, and the unemployment office treated non-English speakers with impatience, adding another layer to our struggle. My childhood responsibilities included acting as a translator, lacking the vocabulary to express the urgency of our needs.

In a moment of deja vu, I vividly remember seeing my teacher and feeling shame for being in this predicament. To my surprise, so did she. I recall thinking I know why I am here, but what the hell is my teacher doing at the unemployment office, too. She had a job. She was our teacher. I realized she was in line ahead of me or behind me; who the hell knows, because we were both waiting in the maze. She poked her neck out to do a double take at the same time I did. She recognized me and I recognized her. We made eye contact, but didn't say a word. We both turned away in embarrassment knowing we knew each other but were too ashamed to acknowledge each other out loud. This wasn't a pleasant place to be for either of us, so we moved the hell on. In the end, we both knew we were on our own. She probably didn't want to give me an explanation, and I surely didn't want to tell her mine. Although we came from two different paths, we ended up in the same place at the same time. Both of us, for our own reasons, were dealing with the unemployment office workers who didn't want to be there either. I thought damn, life is hard, even for my own teacher. This wasn't isolated to me, my mom, and grandma; this extended beyond. That day, I learned how quickly, through shame, we ignore each other instead of reaching out our hand. It was frustrating all around.

Sights of Self-Sufficiency

I used to sit at the table where my mom had lunch at the factory after school to wait until she clocked out of work. When I was old enough to stay home alone, I recall a single box of macaroni after school felt like a feast. Hunger prompted self-sufficiency. Cooking pasta became a necessity before it was ever a skill. The first attempt shocked my mother when she came home from work fear, relief, and gratitude flickered across her face. Burning the building down was a possibility, but so was starvation. My grandparents and aunts who lived down the hallway had their own commitments, leaving no one at home after school. This was an early lesson in self-reliance. Risking trouble to cook became a reasonable trade-off for a full stomach. No microwave existed, no pocket money, no stocked fridge, only a jar of pasta sauce and a box of macaroni sitting on top of the refrigerator. Occasionally, mayonnaise replaced cheese, creating an unexpected comfort meal. Hunger likely influenced the enjoyment of that odd combination. These days, mayonnaise and my memory hold a distant relationship. This taught me about calculated risks. I learned my own needs could be honored instead of the expectations set by the adults around me. I knew they asked me not to cook out of fear, but I knew that if I was careful, I could trust my choices and be safe. Because

I was old enough to be home alone, I could manage making macaroni. I had seen my mom make it a million times. Not to mention, I was hungry as hell. It would be hours before anyone would be home to make it for me. The hunger was so fierce, I went against the rules, guided by my created guardrails that made the food, ate and didn't burn the apartment building down. My mom was both proud and relieved with a giggle of disbelief. Me, I was like, well, with my chest out like Superman, ah, excuse me, like Superwoman, "What else could I make now besides Holy Macaroni?" (Under supervision of course.)

Scarcity and Personal Identity

Even my identity was compromised by scarcity. Two situations marked my need to conform in school. One was wearing a poofy Mexican dress to school. The kids made so much fun of me because I was overdressed. From my dress to my socks to my hair to my shoes, they laughed at me so hard, which brought such shame and embarrassment. This made me not want to show my cultural identity and my femininity because kids would ridicule me. When I was a little older, the other situation was when sharing everything with my younger brother was the norm. We wore the same Champion black or navy sweaters to school. Personal style or preference held no place in that reality. Being an individual seemed unattainable. My classmates took notice, their passive-aggressive remarks stinging me daily. Shame festered, making school an unbearable experience. Every day in elementary school, the desire to disappear, to never return, grew stronger with each insult. Poverty clung visibly, making it impossible to hide. The question lingers: do people still see that poverty in me today? That occasional question pops up now and again, but now I know who the F*** I am and how those memories helped shape me. I've become powerful because of those experiences. These days I wreak worthiness instead.

Choice Becomes Inevitable

My mother's inability to make her own life choices became one of my greatest life lessons. The realization struck early: different choices were possible. Yet, in her mind, options did not exist. She was a wife and mother, roles that defined her world. More children continued to arrive, deepening an already inescapable struggle. The nightmare persisted, with only fleeting moments of joy. Her experience made the value of choice clear for me. Thoughtful decision-making, with a clear understanding of its purpose and audience, became essential when I contemplated life choices. Most importantly, the lesson of independent pursuit of goals emerged. Her lonely, yet courageous journey from Mexico to the United States at the young age of 15 with six-month old me and her new husband, despite its challenges, illustrated an example of the pursuit for happiness. For me, choosing a different path was an option, a necessity, even. My mother taught me that I could make my own choices because she modeled her strength by leaving Mexico. This meant I could be the creator of my own destiny because she had already endured so much for my sake.

From Survival to Self-Actualization

From the brick-red buildings of a forgotten neighborhood to the revelation of Maslow's hierarchy at age 23, this journey began at "negative zero." My raw story weaves through the complexities of growing up in extreme scarcity, where empty stomachs met empty promises and where survival wasn't just a concept but a daily mandate. Through the lens of my younger self serving as both eldest daughter and family translator, I witnessed the brutal education of street economics: factories that exploited immigrant mothers, unemployment lines that tested dignity, and the harsh reality that being "poor" meant something far more permanent than being "broke."

Yet beneath the surface of this survival story lies a deeper current of transformation. My evolution from sharing Champion sweaters with my brother to recognizing the power of choice marks the beginning of a profound shift. My mother's brave journey from Mexico, though wrapped in struggle, planted the seeds of possibility, showing that even in the most confined circumstances, one could still choose a different path.

My story serves as more than a memoir of hardship; it's a blueprint for understanding how unmet fundamental needs shape our journey toward self-actualization. Through my unflinching examination of my past, I share how the very circumstances that could have defined my limitations instead became the foundation for my resilience and strategic thinking.

I.N.K. Framework

I – Instinct: Trust your gut, it's your greatest business asset.

N – Navigation: Learn the rules, then rewrite them strategically.

K – Killer Mindset: Own your presence, dominate your lane.

Self-Audit Your Foundation: Take inventory of your four fundamental needs (physiological, safety, belonging, self-esteem). Like the author's revelation through Maslow's hierarchy, understanding where you stand is the first step toward building upward. Create a personal assessment of each level, noting both strengths and gaps that need attention. On www.MiriamSimon.online you will find the three (3) bonuses to serve as your companion to work alongside you on this experience. Obtain an opportunity to hear from me directly and a quick start guide. Get bonuses here.

Transform Scarcity into Strategy: Identify three areas in your life where you've experienced scarcity (whether financial, emotional, or professional). Following the author's path, document how each challenge forced you to develop specific skills or insights. These are your unique assets, the street wisdom that sets you apart in any arena.

Map Your Choice Points: Just as the author recognized her power to make different choices than her mother, create a decision matrix for your next major life or career move. List the options that might not be obvious at first glance, especially those that challenge your inherited beliefs about what's possible.

P.E.A.R.L.S. Strategy

These early experiences of scarcity and survival taught me the foundation of what would later evolve into my P.E.A.R.L.S. strategy for success. While I.N.K. helped me survive, P.E.A.R.L.S. would eventually transform my survival skills into strategic power positioning myself where opportunity could find me, executing with excellence, adapting to setbacks, building resilience while celebrating small wins, leveraging every relationship, and ultimately claiming my sovereignty in spaces never designed for people "like me."

LEARNING TO FIGHT

How Brushes with Death
Taught Me to Live

The realization that your life could be over in an instant really does change your frame of thought, the decisions you make, the people you surround yourself with, and the amount of bullshit you tolerate. Sometimes you let go of places. Sometimes you let go of previous ways of thinking, previous perceptions, previous ways of living. When sh*t hits the fan, all you know is that you just need to change. Something has to give. Something has to go differently. Things need to be different. All the time, in every circumstance, the one person you can control is you. Everybody else will stay where they are until they're ready to move on; until they're ready to do what they need to do, and unfortunately, once you realize that, it's the end. It makes it difficult to move on but not doing so is worse. For me, I recognize the value of being alive, because of so many times death has visited me. I can see each experience all too clearly, as if they all just happened a few seconds ago and I will share a few of them with you so that you can think about your own life and maybe think twice about how you see it or take a second to say the hell with the past and move the f*ck on.

I've been hit with a few pivotal moments in my life where life and death had such an impact. One that I remember truly vividly is when I was a young kid, and I was just standing in the kitchen deciding whether I wanted to end my life or not. All I can remember is looking at the white fridge and looking at the knife that was there and for

27

many seconds, maybe minutes, I was just looking and thinking, looking and thinking, looking and thinking going back-and-forth in my head. I can recall vividly how I hated my life. Yes, hated. I know it's a strong word, but that's how I felt. How much I did not want to be there. How I wish I was elsewhere. How I wish my life was different. How I wish all the BS could just disappear. How people could just disappear and I just wish my life was completely different.

I don't quite recall what exactly made me change my mind, but all I know is I made a decision not to go through with it, and that decision has meant everything, because although my life was hectic, my life was ridiculously harsh. My life was being a poor little Mexican girl in a new town in a new area in a new place where I just didn't fit in. Where I didn't know where I was, where I didn't know where I stood and I didn't know how to move forward I just knew that I didn't want to die. I don't recall many things from my childhood because I'd rather not think about them. I'd rather remove them from my memory. I'd rather not talk to anybody about them. I'd rather act like it didn't exist, and I'd rather just ignore that past. If I could erase those years of my life, I probably would. If I could wish a wish it would be to have all those memories gone and all those disgusting moments disappear because during my early childhood I recall living one of the worst times of my life, not being happy, being in my head, being in my mind, fighting people from beating me up, and being so different I didn't even have friends. Being so different that people looked at me weird. Being so poor that people made fun of me. Being so little that people would pick on me. It was a time when all I knew was that I needed to square up. I needed to

28

be strong. I needed to fend for myself, by myself. In order to survive, I needed to fight. I didn't have any food. I didn't have any money. I didn't have parents along my side to advocate for me. I didn't have people who supported me. No big sister or brother to protect me. I was the big sister, in a small package with minimal resources. Everybody was trying to find their way and everybody was trying to make ends meet and all I could think about was why am I in this stupid mess. How could I get out of it? What can I do to remove myself from this type of life? That's why I kept contemplating my life or lack thereof. I weighed my options, looking at my veins and thinking maybe I should do it but I didn't. One of the worst things sometimes, is to know that there are times where you have to let it happen. You can't do anything because you're so young. You're so vulnerable. You're just a kid. They tell you not to get involved in adult matters. Don't do this, don't do that. All I wanted was to be a kid. Unfortunately, I didn't have an outlet, yet.

The Day Laughter Turned to Silence

One of the happiest moments of my life came during my teenage years, between 13 and 17, playing volleyball at the court two blocks from our building. My grandparents had a little more money for us that they'd buy my brother & I one pair of Nike sneakers that were on sale a year to play at the gym in school and show off at the local park. After school each day, the sport became my sanctuary playing with adults, feeling the rush of competition, finding pure joy in every serve and spike.

The park became my home away from home. Mexican day parades, basketball tournaments, volleyball tournaments, soccer tournaments, neighborhood kids gathering, and forging connections. Among these faces, one person stood out. Our friendship blossomed naturally, despite him being about six years older. We shared an effortless bond. We were always there for each other. Especially enjoyed his infectious humor. People often remarked how much he resembled Robert De Niro with identical moles and similar hair.

His playfulness knew no bounds. Sometimes he'd call my grandparents' phone number 973-778-2215, a number forever etched in my memory and he'd giggle, "Look out the window." Standing a whole block away from his 4-story building at the corner of Market and Essex Streets in Passaic, NJ he'd wave intensely and with the widest smile, prompting laughter and of course he'd receive my returned greetings from my window of my 4-story red brick building on the corner of Market and Bergen Streets. Those were the best types of calls. It was always greeted with the same infectious laughter and joy.

Our closeness evolved naturally. Sharing everything about our lives, enjoying each other's company so completely that eventually, he became my boyfriend. His caring nature and unprecedented trust manifested in ways never before experienced, entrusting his entire paycheck on Fridays, lending his favorite leather coat in the winter and his favorite Nautica jacket in the Spring. We shared secrets about our exes & family that nobody else knew. Our friendship transcended ordinary boundaries.

Unfortunately, our time together proved fleeting. My mother constantly questioned his presence, wondering why he always came around. Her disapproval emerged through harsh comments: "Hope he disappears." "Hope he leaves you." "Hope he stops talking to you." My mother and I were never aligned; we rarely found harmony. Her concerns were dismissed with my ignorance and my teenage indifference: "Just leave me alone. He's fine. Nothing is wrong with him. There's nothing going on." She, like many others, could see our synchronicity and our untimely fate.

Then came that fateful day at the billiards place on the same block he lived on; one block from home for me. The place we hung out at when we were not at the park. The place most said, girls don't belong there, but I enjoyed playing pool. I was actually really good at it. They often called me a shark because they had no idea how good I was until they played me or played us. While playing pool, some neighborhood guys entered, looked around, and then left. I felt there was something up. The guys in the pool hall gathered. I inquired, what's going on. My friend told me, "hey, they are coming for me. Don't worry. Everything will be okay." The truth. It wasn't. Within minutes, as we walked toward the door to check if they had left to see if it was clear to leave, to get home, gunshots suddenly rang out directly at us. In an instant without me even seeing, he pushed me out of harm's way and I heard his body fall. Turning to check on him, the horrifying sight of blood flowing from his chest confirmed my worst fears. At this moment, I knew it was the end. Why? A few weeks prior, playfully punching him in the chest caused him to lose his breath due to a previous stab wound unknown to me at the time. Seeing

31

the shotgun wound in the exact location, deep down, the knowledge that this wouldn't end well settled in.

The memories of that day remain fragmented. Everything happened with dizzying speed. At just 17 years old, I spent the night in the police station, and the morning brought the devastating news that he didn't survive. My uncle came to give me the news.

Previous hardships paled in comparison to this tragedy. Life turned upside down in an instant. Before that day, he had been like the mayor of our neighborhood beloved by all. People gravitated toward his jokes, his unique ability to bring others together and talk sense into troublemakers. Calm, smart, hardworking yet he became another statistic, a casualty of our surroundings and circumstances.

Until that moment, life had been mostly fun and games. Despite past difficulties, true friendship had finally been found. Prior experiences with sadness couldn't compare to the cold emptiness that followed. Days passed lying on the bottom bunk shared with my sister, unable to move or face the world.

The aftermath brought unexpected isolation. Former friends disappeared, unwilling to be involved or learn what happened. Speculation ran rampant, with people creating their own versions of events. Some even seemed to blame me for surviving while he was gone. The confusion was overwhelming. There was no understanding of why it happened, no clue about what was going on. Only the crushing reality that he was gone forever.

This moment changed my perspective of life. It showed me the cowardness in people, the heart of others, the jealousy from others, and also the deception of a selective few. It gave me the sense that life can be over at any moment. It showed me life is short. It showed me past wounds, when retouched hurt, sometimes even end us. On the other side of the spectrum, it signified a new path forward, a new beginning. An opportunity to live that was short lived for him, but not for me. It brought the responsibility to make his sacrifice worthwhile. It gave me strength, hope and endless possibilities. It showed me love. It showed me true friendship. It gave me life.

When Faith Outlasts Fear: A Mother's Vigil

Admittedly, youth, vulnerability and ignorance colored every decision. Shortly after losing my friend, I met someone who would turn my life another 180 degrees. At 18, fresh out of high school, balancing a new job and college classes, falling into what seemed like love at the moment led to the birth of my first-born son, Samuel. Nearly losing him began at 24 weeks of pregnancy when labor started unexpectedly. My water breaking at home prompted a rushed hospital visit. Young and naive, the severity of the situation of a baby 12 weeks early remained unclear to me.

Confined to bed rest in the hospital, Samuel received lung-developing medication through a stomach injection. Shortly after, an ambulance transfer from the local facility to one with specialized doctors followed.

Thankfully, despite my inexperience, our friendly doctor made all the right moves.

In retrospect, stress had accumulated difficulties with my mother and my boyfriend, plus a workplace incident. Bed rest continued until Samuel arrived at 26 weeks, weighing 5 pounds and 2 ounces, surprisingly large for his gestational age. His extended hospital stay marked the first time doctors warned of possible mortality.

Every winter for three years brought renewed hope against threatening circumstances. By age 2½, Samuel became fatally ill as winter descended, with his third birthday approaching in Spring. By then, my second child, Rosa, had joined the family. Looking at pictures from that period now prompts disbelief, somehow surviving those moments through a peculiar calm born of youthful ignorance or an undeniable faith, never truly contemplating the nearness of death.

Hospital visits became cyclical that winter through February discharged only to return; released only to be readmitted. Eventually, the doctor delivered grave news: Samuel might not reach his third birthday on March 11. The illness had progressed beyond identification, manifesting in allergic reactions and skin ailments abscesses, deadened tissue with horrific odor. What began as RSV (respiratory syncytial virus) led to lung collapse, with intubation as the final option. His pediatrician, Dr Sarigul, the sweetest, most caring and knowledgeable doctor, imaginable exhausted every possibility, recommended specialists, and explained how intubation would support breathing while his body recuperated.

Then came a pivotal moment: a surgical gamble to remove Samuel's tonsils, with uncertain results. The situation grew so dire that a priest visited, offering his prayers for both a young mother and a grave child. Days and nights passed in constant vigil beside the bed in the ICU.

During one of those nights, a horrific event unfolded while Samuel recuperated from surgery. A toddler rushed into the ICU accompanied by a police officer, always a troubling sign. The ICU layout, with beds around the perimeter and a central nurses' station for monitoring, offered no privacy from overhearing the child's situation. He had been beaten so severely that survival seemed unlikely. And unlikely came true; the little boy ultimately passed away overnight, apparently without parental presence. This tragedy struck me deeply, the juxtaposition of fighting for one child's life while another departed this world alone, mistreated, with only police as escort.

My deep faith remained a constant companion throughout my life's challenges. Even with overwhelming odds against Samuel's health: intubation, breathing assistance, allergic reactions, and four months of hospitalization. The belief in his recovery never wavered. The thought of losing my little boy, premature but strong, simply couldn't take root. The nursing staff, who became familiar faces to us, commended my maternal strength and suggested taking breaks, which were refused out of my dedication to monitoring his care.

After prolonged intubation, Dr. Sarigul began weaning Samuel off sedation. Witnessing his discomfort while returning to consciousness with tears flowing out of his eyes, down his face without hearing his voice brought me mixed emotions, heartbreaking to see pain in a two-year-old, yet reassuring to observe emotional responses after complete sedation, which was a complete miracle. Mercifully, post-surgery recovery proved complete, ending the cycle of winter hospitalizations.

This chapter amplified an ongoing journey of resilience. Despite having no control over Samuel's health, faith and trust in his medical team remained unshaken. Twenty-six years later, the bald spot on the back of his head persists as a permanent reminder of his extended hospital bed confinement. This marking symbolizes not just nearly losing a little boy, but the remarkable calm, fighting spirit within him.

Against All Odds: A Mother's Intuition

Before meeting my second born, Rosa, a profound message from the womb demanded trust she was beyond ready to live a full life! So eager, in fact, that at just twenty weeks of pregnancy, she attempted to make an early appearance. The problem: her development remained incomplete. During this period over twenty years ago, ultrasounds were just beginning to reveal the gender and confirm her normal development. Unfortunately, the doctor's call requesting an immediate visit carried worrying news. Several abnormalities appeared in her ultrasound: fingers of uneven size, multiple cysts, and smaller-than-normal dimensions.

The prognosis suggested high chances of Down Syndrome, with pregnancy termination offered as an option. Before finalizing any decision, confirmation through womb sampling remained possible, though the procedure itself carried significant risk of triggering premature labor.

The news landed on me with numbing shock. With risks accompanying either path, the less dangerous option needed careful consideration. At merely 19 years old, facing a decision between testing for illness and potentially terminating the pregnancy weighed heavily. Then came a miracle or perhaps divine intervention. An inexplicable motherly instinct awakened with Rosa's first movements. Following the concerning diagnosis, her activity became constant and unmistakable. This seemed the perfect sign to delay the procedure temporarily. Youth and minimal family history of Down Syndrome suggested favorable odds, despite the identified abnormalities. The compassionate sonogram technician noticed my concern and encouraged my thoughtful decision-making. Her kindness resonated deeply with me speaking directly to me as a woman to another woman during the appointments typically attended alone.

While patience seemed the wisest approach, Rosa harbored different plans. Contractions began shortly after the diagnosis and continued through week 36! Medical disbelief dismissed these sensations as mere discomfort. To me, the unfamiliar pressure and light sensations warranted explanation. Once again, pregnancy meant balancing work with recurring hospital visits. My determination to save my daughter fueled persistence until the doctor finally provided overnight contraction monitoring confirming the unbelievable truth. After the analysis, immediate bed rest followed, with self-administered injections every three days to protect the pregnancy.

Rosa ultimately reached full term, allowing for scheduled childbirth, which brought me the most excruciating physical pain imaginable. The entire hospital likely heard those simultaneous screams and cries, balanced with attempts to maintain enough composure to complete labor. The epidural proved ineffective, with no time for additional medication, leaving no choice but to endure the process. This moment also promised long-awaited answers about Rosa's health. Deep intuition suggested wellness, though uncertainty remained. After enduring ultimate physical suffering, the doctors delivered the joyous news that a beautiful, healthy girl had arrived, full of fighting spirit! Gratitude overflowed my heart & spirit that despite facing two separate threats to her survival, maternal instinct and unwavering faith resulted in the presence of my charming, beautiful daughter.

I have learned so much from my daughter Rosa, but this sincerely brought me the ability to advocate for myself. I knew deep inside that I was feeling contractions. I knew I was going into labor at 20 weeks of pregnancy. I knew from my son, who came early at 26 his chances of survival were minimal, so imagine her at an even earlier time, 6 weeks earlier. There was no way I would not speak up knowing what I knew, what I felt, and what the consequences could be if left unsaid.

The Fight Continues

Life has thrown me against the wall repeatedly, from contemplating suicide as a poor Mexican girl in a strange town, to watching my best friend take a bullet that could have been mine, to nearly losing both my children before I even got to know them. Through each encounter with death, I've gained something invaluable: the fierce determination to live fully and authentically.

Those moments when everything hangs in the balance strip away the bullshit. When I stood in that kitchen as a child, staring at a knife, something deep inside whispered to keep going. When I heard my friend's body hit the ground after pushing me from harm's way, I inherited not just his sacrifice but his spirit. When doctors told me my children might not survive, my intuition burned brighter than their statistics.

The street doesn't lie, and neither does death. Both have taught me that survival isn't just about breathing, it's about claiming your right to exist exactly as you are. The wisdom I've earned through blood, tears, and sheer stubborn will isn't taught in boardrooms or business schools, but it's exactly what's needed to navigate both worlds successfully.

What separates those who merely exist from those who truly live is this: when life knocks you down, you don't just get up, you come back stronger, wiser, and more determined to make every heartbeat count. My tattoos are my scars, my pearls are my victories, and together they make me unstoppable.

I.N.K. Framework

Honor Your Battle-Tested Instinct: Write down three moments when your gut saved you while everyone else thought you were crazy. Those weren't flukes, they were your instinct speaking. Next time you face resistance in the boardroom or on the street, remember how that same instinct has kept you alive. Your intuition isn't just an asset; it's your superpower when you're brave enough to listen.

Create Your Strategic Navigation Map: Identify where you've been playing small because of other people's limitations. Just as I pushed through hospital bureaucracy when my children's lives depended on it, outline three situations where you need to rewrite the rules instead of following them. Remember, sometimes the most strategic path isn't the one everyone else is taking, it's the one only you can see.

Develop Your Killer Mindset Daily Practice: Each morning, remind yourself what you've already survived. The bullets that missed you. The odds you've overcome. When I almost lost my children, I didn't have the luxury of doubt. List five impossible circumstances you've already conquered, and carry them with you into every meeting, negotiation, and challenge. When you've stared down death, corporate intimidation tactics become laughable.

Remember, your power doesn't come from fitting in, it comes from surviving when the world bet against you. Those tattoos under your business suit aren't contradictions; they're your credentials. Wear them proudly.

P.E.A.R.L.S. Strategy

These brushes with death didn't just change me, they forged the P.E.A.R.L.S. strategy I now offer you as your path to power without compromise. When I stood frozen in that kitchen contemplating suicide, watched my friend take a bullet meant for both of us, and fought through medical systems to save my children, I wasn't just surviving, I was unconsciously mastering the art of Positioning myself as someone who refuses to be dismissed, executing with unwavering determination when others said to give up, Adapting to impossible circumstances while maintaining my core truth, building Resilience through trauma while learning to Reward myself for each victory, Leveraging every resource and relationship available (like that compassionate sonogram technician who spoke woman-to-woman), and ultimately claiming my Sovereignty by trusting my instincts over external authorities. The streets taught me that when life gives you impossible choices, like whether to test for Down Syndrome with potentially devastating consequences, you don't just follow protocols; you rewrite them based on the intelligence your life experiences have given you.

CONCRETE RUNWAYS

Taking Flight from Urban Lessons to Corporate Heights

"Mirror, Mirror on the wall, I'll always get up after I fall. Whether I run, walk, or crawl, I will set my goals & achieve them all."
- Chris Butler @WomenWhoLeadEmpires

Admitting my many areas of brokenness was a huge pill to swallow. Coming from a broken family then creating the same; being "la del pasaporte verde", instead of having the blue American passport, putting on display my displacement, showing my inability to speak the language and understand the customs; living with a full heart of betrayal; becoming a young mother who had very little experience and resources to raise my children; waking up with a faint far-fetched hope; and showcasing the body that had attracted ill intent.

Living in brokenness is all I knew to be true for most of my life. I felt like a mirror that was broken into a million pieces that at times were scattered all over the place, waiting to be found to be reconnected to their home base, but every time I tried, the puzzle piece I'd pick up was the wrong piece, trying to embrace the next piece incorrectly. At other times, a couple of pieces full of energy that were ready to face the world, failed miserably, only to be broken further all over again. There were gaps of missing pieces full of black holes that ventured into nothingness, other pieces were tarnished with harmful wounds, while other shreds were holding on to regenerative healing and hope.

When I look back at my brokenness, it automatically makes me close my eyes shut tight, shed endless tears in sadness, and make my long eyelashes splash away the tears. The internal eternal darkness from where my brokenness started was a difficult place from which to show up in life. My internal compass was directionless in the admittance of the hurt that lived in my chest. My core trembled to keep me standing up and not fall to the ground. My mind circled in an entranced daze, not thinking about anything but empty in sorrow. The power with which the brokenness would hold me back and down was a force too big for me to go at alone, at times; at other times, I had no choice but to find the strength to push through it to get beyond it.

Grandma's Lesson in Brokenness

One of the most influential individuals in my life is my grandma Ofelia because she saw me in a way that others can't fathom to understand. They do say a grandmother's love is one of a kind and now I completely understand that love with my own granddaughter Lily who came into our lives at the perfect time to re-invite joy and brightness back into our home after losing my beloved mother-in-law Betsy. Interestingly, Lily and I share a similar bond that I did with my grandmother Ofelia. She was one of my greatest teachers, cheerleaders, and magical guides in life.

A moment of clarity in brokenness happened when she broke her right wrist while taking my brother and me sledding. Throughout my childhood, each year, my grandpa Porfirio, the only one of the two who could drive, took my brother and me wherever they went, but especially to the different parks in the area. On this cold day, after a snow storm, we bundled up and jumped into my grandpa's van to make our way to the park located across the street from the famous Hot Grill in Clifton, NJ, A 50-year-old fast-food joint with incredible Texas hot dogs, burgers & sandwiches. Nash Park had a high hill perfect for sledding, and many neighborhood kids went there. In retrospect, sledding was the start of me loving the thrill of being free and fast, unstoppable, and building more momentum the further I went. In the Spring, I would enjoy closing my eyes, smelling the fresh grass and flowers, and the heat of the shining sun rolling down the same hill.

In the winter, we enjoyed joyriding across town to go sledding. After a day of fun and exhilaration as we departed the park walking the long, cold, icy sidewalk back to the van, my grandmother slipped, fell, and hurt her hand. She went to the hospital, and we anxiously awaited her return, and they gave us the news that she had broken her wrist. We were so sad to see her in pain and unable to be the feisty, quick-witted grandma who would cook for the entire family on weekends, rush out the door Monday through Friday, only to realize one flight down the stairs, she had two different shoes on and return running back to look for the matching shoe all while laughing about the entire thing. I had no idea that this event would lead to building a greater bond with my grandmother. As the oldest granddaughter, I spent a lot of time at my grandparents' apartment, which was just down the hallway. My grandmother would require an extra set of hands to do almost everything.

One of the places I loved the most was my grandmother's kitchen. It was small & cozy, full of interesting conversations, laughter, and always filled with Mexican hot chocolate or cafe de oya aromatics. I now do the same in our kitchen with my wife Kerry, but now enjoy the homemade Puerto Rican specialty dishes she makes with her very own sofrito.

Becoming my grandmother's right hand until her wrist was fully operational was not in my plans, but it was a rewarding experience. Complementing my grandma's moves by helping make dinner and doing chores around the house after school and on weekends was a heart-warming time of my life. We had so many laughs, sometimes to the point our stomachs hurt that interrupted and delayed the accomplishment of our tasks. Grandma had so much patience with a young girl who really had no experience with anything in the kitchen besides the occasional macaroni. It was no small feat to learn to make typical Mexican dishes like yellow rice, beans from scratch, and other delicacies because everyone loved her food - not mine, but we gave it a go. Being on her team was the greatest way she showed me that although the usefulness of her hand was out of commission, due to the broken bones, by collaborating with me, a novice, and patient, we could accomplish the same or even more because now my own flair was added to it. The lessons learned were invaluable to me and I thank her every day because the outcome was the more people worked together, the more we had, and the more we could do and be.

You Won't be First and You Be the Last

After creating the life my mom had, choosing to walk away from it was the answer. Another lesson that was pivotal in my brokenness was my grandmother's advice after leaving the apartment I had rented from my aunt Gloria with my two kids and unknowingly expecting my third child. I needed to create space between the jerk that I trusted with my heart. My grandmother's advice at the kitchen table was, "You're going to be okay, you're not the first, and you won't be the last." She saw my struggle with a broken heart, my broken family, and my knowing that it was best to part ways for my own happiness and that of my children. This conversation changed the trajectory of my life forever. Although it took me some time to completely separate from him, about two more years, we were on our path to better days. The physical boundary of moving where he had to face my grandparents and my grandfather's mean huff and puff that included, "This guy again, come on my friend" in his broken English, which meant seriously, you again, I'm sick of you, get away from her. My eyes would open wide, and my eyebrows would do a high rise along with my teeth grinding just thinking of how much my grandpa disliked this guy with reason. The discomfort my kid's father brought to our lives is what made me reiterate what I knew already - get as far away from this guy as you can; he had done enough damage.

My grandmother's words were so impactful to me that they gave me the strength to be able to make the decision to be at peace without him. Deep down, I knew my life would be better. Deep down, I knew I needed to be a better person for my son, my daughter, and my unborn child. When my grandmother said those words, I was already expecting my third child. My unborn child brought me so much peace. I was able to move on from my broken relationship because I had learned that my baby could feel what I felt. I knew that being upset, riddled with anxiety, would only lead to a path of more despair and a complicated pregnancy. My choice to set the boundary to stay away from their father proved fruitful because I had a relatively easy pregnancy. I had such a deep connection with each of my three kids. This time, the connection was even deeper because I was able to experience being pregnant without chaos. I went to full term, worked throughout my entire pregnancy, drove myself to each doctor's visit, and drove myself to the hospital when I was ready to give birth. No one accompanied me. I decided not to find out the gender to keep it a surprise and be excited the day I saw my newborn baby. I wanted to look forward to the day. And I did. I had no names prepared. All the baby's clothes were yellow. I kept it really simple and basic. But basic, was not what happened at the hospital. From one moment to the next, the baby was ready to make their appearance. So much so that our doctor didn't make it in time to deliver the baby. The resident doctor flew in to deliver the baby. They asked me, "Are you all alone?." I replied, "yes, it's only me and you all." Within the next twenty minutes, without any epidurals, I gave birth to a beautiful healthy girl. On our first look, her name popped out at me, because she gave me a mischievous look; I welcomed my daughter Mitzi to the world. For many years, she was like my twin. We looked so much alike.

Although the brokenness was a difficult one to face because it involved three Precious Moments, my first-born son Samuel, second born Rosa and Mitzi. They are only a year and four months apart. People used to think my first two were twins because they not only looked alike but were close in age. The path forward was a difficult one, I was not really ready for. The thought of what people would say about a 21-year-old with three kids frightened me. There were people who definitely judged me. Some people would ask me questions like: were they all from the same dad? The nerve of people to question who their father was. My answer to them would be to simply walk away. Wow, the bias towards a young mother, instead of being of help, they were more judgmental than supportive. The goal wasn't for my kids to be fatherless like me, nor give them a deadbeat father like mine, but here I was faced with that reality. Throughout those years, freedom was gained day by day. My kids became my priority. They were the gift of life; the one miracle that came out of that motherhood relationship. The relationship was only a season and not a permanent relationship. Although brokenhearted, I learned that true unconditional love came into my life from my trio who gave me a second chance at love.

This quote gave me the perspective to think, you're right, grandma, I don't need to be the last even if I am the first. This transcended into my ability to multiply my efforts, thinking on a larger scale and forge the future state with people who could carry out the same I started.

48

Alignment With the "Navigation" Component of the I.N.K. Framework

Facing death gave me a different perspective on life. I not only knew that life could be over, but that if it is over, death changes everything. The same is not the same any longer. Facing death requires facing life, and whether or not you are actually living it.

Every time I think about the smiles, fun, and joy I miss from my friend who died when I was 17, I don't want to wonder what having fun, living with joy, or being happy is like. I live my life! I didn't survive to live a small life, to live a life of stress, to live a life of darkness. I survived to be me without doubts, and to love my life. Deep down, this has been my driving force to stay positive, to listen to my gut, to listen to the whispers of life that speak to me, and to enjoy my life.

I have innately believed in myself. I know that whatever I dedicate myself to, I will be able to make it into the best. Not because I think I am better than anyone else, but because I can make something from nothing. I knew I would be a sought-after employee if I dedicated myself to understanding the business better than anyone else. It would be impossible for people not to consider me when opportunities presented themselves. I never did anything to get anything in return, but the law of abundance works in bountiful ways.

If you have never heard of the law of abundance, you should become familiar with it because it states that there's an unlimited supply of resources, wealth, and opportunities available to everyone. I lived an early life of scarcity, so following the law of abundance meant living my life to the fullest. This mindset changed my trajectory. When I learned that I could have everything I've ever wanted in life and that my life was out there for me to live, I just kept going. I stayed the course. I took the path less traveled, which, by the way, I loved Robert Frost's poem "The Road Not Taken" since the first time I read it in elementary school. I also live my leadership style that way because, "taking the path less traveled has made all the difference." I waited patiently for a big break, and the day finally came. "Get me on that roller coaster because I am ready to go; go get it!"

At my job at the airport, I could have easily stayed within the ranks of customer service representative, and there is nothing wrong with that, but it wasn't in the cards for me to stay there. There was a reason I remained the constant in that company while managers came in and went out. I grew leaps and bounds by doing something for so long. Although a constant for almost 15 years, I never stayed the same; I grew professionally. I did not know it back then, but the preparation I received led me to where I am today. The funny part is that I did not think I would be where I am today a decade ago, but I knew there was a life to live, and I was ready to go for it.

When I began my new role in a different organization, I knew a few people who had left and joined this group. I recognized that they doubled their salaries in 5 years. So, I made it my business to do the same. One thing about me is that I learn from other people. Why should I not model what others are doing to accomplish my goals? I do not copy them, I model them, which is different & important. People can smell fakes from anywhere, and from where I come, you don't want to be fake. The way I analyzed things was my way because it had to resonate with me and be right for me. I also can't stand to get things without earning them. The value I bring is so powerful that I know it takes work and that my results speak for themselves.

Like anything I have ever done, I was faced with two crossroads. Right before I joined this organization, I was interviewed for two different roles: an entry-level role and a supervising role. However, the salary was not that much different. I had to review my options, and I took the one less traveled, which was to take the entry-level position. Why? Because it was the better of the two choices for me. I already knew that I qualified for the supervising position, and I could make more money when I arrived there. It was also in a department that was much smaller, wasn't in my expertise wheelhouse, and I would be doing more as a supervisor, making almost the same as the entry-level position. Something was a bit off there, and I was not taking the bait.

Making this decision was the best I ever made. However, I did not love the job right away. I had been a one-woman show handling a million things, and now I was handling a portion of the work. I was working about an hour a day, although this job was considered a full-time job. I just did this job quickly, and I had a lot of time to wander. I took advantage of the time. I did three things that put me on the path to future success. First, I learned about the organization, which had many different departments and was spread out across two states in NJ

& NY. Second, I began to take advantage of the benefits they offered. And third, I did not miss an opportunity for promotion.

Understanding the organization you work for is key to understanding where you stand, where you can go, and how the business operates. If you do not know the company's tag line, you have some work to do. Just like curious George, it's in my nature to be curious, and I like to get to know the ins and outs of organizations. This has helped me find gaps that, when matched with my expertise, I can find and offer solutions, making me a key player within any organization. Some people see problems, but I see opportunities to make things better. I see innovation. This is a super business power skill that any leader or organization would want on their team. Every business has gaps, and they are in need of people who can find the best ways to manage those gaps. During my first six months, I learned about the organization, who the contacts were, and the different departments and populations it served.

The world is full of opportunities, and you need to be ready to meet the moment. This is where I learned that my organization had tuition reimbursement. This was a benefit I had waited for. For 15 years! I always knew I'd get my degree, but unfortunately, I left that dream on hold when I was faced with choosing to raise my son rather than continue school and simultaneously work. Unfortunately, I had to sacrifice college, but here I was faced with the opportunity to finish what I started. By the fall in my first year with the organization, I began my adult learning journey, which was a difficult trip, but well worth the hike.

Simultaneously, my coworker had a medical emergency and was out of work for a prolonged period of time, which gave me the opportunity to do more and learn another job quickly, which was always preparing me for my future role. Taking on the additional role opened the gates to learning and understanding the collective bargaining agreements within the organization. I had worked with one of them already in my previous role, so I was ready to tap into that knowledge like nothing. Now, I added several more union agreements knowledge to my plate, which was such an impactful learning experience.

Becoming a well-rounded professional was always the key, but it was the road less traveled to get there. During my first few years, I missed an opportunity for advancement because I listened to someone who explained I was too new to go for it, which was a massive mistake. Talking about mistakes, I know as a leadership coach that nothing is a mistake. Everything is an experience that teaches us something. I learned to apply to positions regardless of people's opinions. I missed another opportunity because I did not have the degree yet, and they would not replace the job qualifications with experience. I ended up doubling up on my courses, which was against the university's recommendations, but I was not going to let anyone tell me what I could or could not do. And guess what? I did!

When I was taking on extra work and doing more, I recalled the law of attraction, which means that you are drawn to things and people that complement you, and whatever you focus on and give your energy to will come back to you. My focus was to learn as much as I could, get my degree, do what others weren't willing to do, and find solutions. I am now sitting in an Executive role within my organization, leading great initiatives and impacting the workforce tremendously. So what does this mean for you, the reader?   Remember, even though the old saying is "The money will come." It is still important to consider that you are compensated appropriately if you work tirelessly for your company. Long are the days when women work twice as hard and earn less. If women want to lessen the wage disparities in the workforce, we must know our value and get paid our worth.

I.N.K. Framework

Instinct: Trust your inner wisdom about when to create boundaries. My body would physically react to brokenness - my "core trembling," my mind in a "daze" - signals I eventually learned to recognize. When my grandfather huffed and puffed at my ex's presence, it reinforced what I already knew inside: "get far away from this guy." Honor these physical and emotional responses as your internal guidance system, even when you can't fully articulate why.

Navigation: Find mentors and allies who can help chart a path through difficulty. My grandmother became my compass when I felt "directionless." Working as her "right hand" after her injury taught me the power of collaboration to overcome limitations. When facing judgment as a young mother of three, I focused on my children as my "priority" rather than others' opinions. Create physical boundaries (like moving to my grandparents') when needed to establish distance from toxic situations.

Killer Mindset: Transform brokenness into building blocks for a better future. Like pieces of a broken mirror that needed reconnecting, I learned to integrate my painful experiences into a stronger whole. Remember that difficult seasons are temporary, not permanent. My "broken family" eventually gave me the gift of "true unconditional love" through my children. Use limitations as opportunities to develop new strengths, just as I developed cooking skills while helping my injured grandmother.

P.E.A.R.L.S. Strategy

From brokenness to strength exemplifies bouncing back stronger after challenges, using family wisdom as leverage, and developing sovereignty by eventually walking away from a harmful relationship. The grandmother's broken wrist story specifically illustrates how limitations can be overcome through collaboration and adaptation, creating a perfect foundation for the street-smart wisdom that underpins the entire P.E.A.R.L.S. framework.

BOUNDARIES TO FREEDOM

A Journey of Resilience

We are born into stories not of our choosing. Some enter the world wrapped in narratives of nurturing support, while others arrive amid chapters of absence, turmoil, and pain. This is a story of the latter, a testament to the human capacity to rewrite a legacy of parental absence and dysfunction into one of personal triumph.

What follows is not merely an account of family fracture, but an exploration of how the boundaries we establish, particularly with those who should love us most, can become the very foundations of our freedom. It chronicles a path from childhood confusion to adult clarity, from inherited chaos to intentional peace, and from seeking external validation to discovering internal strength.

This journey illuminates how we can transmute the most painful experiences into wisdom that serves not only our healing but also guides others facing similar struggles. Through therapy, self-reflection, and unwavering determination, the impossible becomes possible: creating wholeness from fragmentation, stability from chaos, and love from its absence.

As you read these pages, you may recognize echoes of your own story or gain insights into experiences vastly different from your own. Either way, the invitation remains the same: to witness how boundaries, rather than walls of isolation, can become the essential architecture of personal freedom and authentic connection.

The Call to Adventure

My father was and continues to be incarcerated. A litany of crimes and toxic behavior landed him in his predicament. My mother, distant and emotionally unavailable due to her circumstances, meant that both parents were absent figures in my life. Support from either remains nonexistent. Yet here I am, against all odds, still sharing my journey. The healing journey began many moons ago when trusting others was an uphill battle, and acceptance from my mother was a need yearned for but known deep down inside would never arrive. Relationships with parents rarely surface in conversation. Most cannot fathom life without parental presence, yet moving forward meant severing these ties. Achieving life's true purpose required surrounding myself with people capable of showing the love felt and still feeling in the heart. This journey to emotionally disconnect from both parents was necessary. It may not be for you, but for some, it is one that must be journeyed alone.

Reality demanded accepting personal power to distinguish between those who mean well and those who don't. Years attempting to change the situation proved futile. Some things remain as they are; choices belong to those unwilling to change for the better. Accepting and respecting those choices became necessary for growth. Continued association with both parents would have simply mirrored their choices and attitudes because birds of a feather flock together.

Experiencing my mother's lack of family support taught valuable lessons about being there for loved ones. With no one from her tribe to turn to in the United States, she endured immense suffering. Her emotional support system became me and, later, my siblings. Understanding her journey brings empathy; however, this does not necessitate remaining tied to someone unwilling, perhaps without realizing, to grow and evolve.

Crossing the Threshold

The most healing decision in life was attending therapy. Growing up in instability led to the development of a fearful-avoidant attachment style, affecting interactions in leadership, marriage, and relationships with children. Recognizing these patterns marked a significant step forward. Unlearning negative, deeply ingrained thoughts allowed for clarity and appropriate shifts in the journey. These negative thoughts, originally designed as protection from past trauma, no longer served a purpose in the present. Thanks to therapy, effective strategies developed to navigate and challenge habitual thought patterns. When triggers arise, conscious effort now breaks those patterns.

Tests, Allies, and Enemies

Slowly but surely, the past sheds page by page, each dragon of trauma slain as it appears. A deep need for familial support remains constant, accompanied by knowledge that it will not materialize in this lifetime. For years, their absence made trust a challenge. Wishing for their support never changed the reality of its scarcity. To this day, acceptance remains out of reach; one parent refuses to acknowledge identity, and the other remains incarcerated. More often than not, self-reliance becomes the only option. This life of scarcity sometimes brings tears, shame, and avoidance. Father's absence created feelings of despair, unworthiness, and insecurity. When present, he brought fear, anxiety, and an endless list of problems needing solutions. The memories remain vivid - painful experiences witnessed as both child and young adult.

The Ordeal

Adding to the chaos, he created another family while still married. His girlfriend and their two daughters became part of the ongoing telenovela unfolding before everyone's eyes. Both my mother and his mistress carried his children simultaneously. My two sisters and two half-sisters are close in age, only months apart, an embarrassment difficult to describe. Yet this forms part of the story witnessed firsthand. My grandparents' decision to accept this situation was baffling, yet they did so simply because my father had nowhere else to go and was their oldest son. The honest truth is they loved my father unconditionally, a reality incomprehensible until becoming a parent myself.

After being exiled from the U.S. for committing a crime, my father returned from Mexico and met his mistress in the hospital after being stabbed. Her name even began with an "F," just like my mother's. The situation wasn't fully understood at the time, but it all played out in plain sight. This woman despised seeing me at my grandparents' house, yet my presence there had been established long before hers. From my perspective, she was the intruder, not me.

More than once, frustration turned into unspoken (and spoken) words. The word "bitch" crossed my mind frequently, and once even escaped the lips after she asked me to leave my grandparents' apartment when no one else was home: "I got here before you, so tough. I'm not leaving." Other times, thoughts like, "Bitch, get a job if you don't want to see me," burned through the mind. Working wasn't an option for me, but she certainly had that choice. Leaving the place that felt like a second home was never an option, and anger burned hot through every interaction.

At the age of seven came the first experience of standing ground by facing people who didn't like me and wanted me gone. Refusal to leave was absolute. We were there together, whether we liked it or not.

The conflict wasn't limited to me. She also fought with my mother. One unforgettable day, they engaged in a physical altercation in the hallway, both pregnant by the same man. It's mind-blowing to think this was reality. Neither woman truly had the love they sought. Whether he cared for both or neither, one thing remained clear: he never respected either of them.

That experience solidified an unshakable truth: never fight over a man. No man is worth that kind of energy. Those who toy with women's hearts aren't worth the battle. The other woman never deserves the pain, but better things exist in life. Looking back now, the lesson wasn't about revenge; clearly, this was just childhood, but about setting boundaries and walking away with dignity, a lesson later embraced as personal truth.

The Revelation

During a recent summit with an incredible coach, participation in an exercise to disconnect from the inner critic revealed something profound. At that moment, recognition dawned that the inner critic had a name: Jackie. Short for Jacqueline, the name my parents almost gave me. The name of my father's first daughter with his then mistress. The daughter he acknowledges. The daughter he loves.

Mourning that fantasy serves no purpose, yet tears still fall like a waterfall when the gates to the inner critic open.

When I was eight, the "gift" of new siblings kept arriving. One day in my thirties, another sibling reached out through Facebook with an introduction: "I'm your brother." He had learned about me through our grandparents in Mexico. In total, there are probably around thirteen of us. No certainty exists because connections with half-siblings were never established. Before, anger stood in the way. Later, personal struggles made it difficult to face their existence. As time passed, the revelations kept coming, alongside the reality that this upbringing was simply that unconventional.

Transformation / Creating My Own Path

Now in my forties, at least no more unexpected messages have appeared. Still, the question lingers: When will the next one come? Despite everything, one truth remains: valuable lessons came from this chaos. My father's actions taught exactly what should never be done. Life is filled with choices, and his path resulted in much pain for many. My mother once claimed strength, intelligence, and resilience might be paternal inheritance. Had life dealt him a different hand or had he played the one he had differently, perhaps another fate would have awaited him. Still, this was the life he chose. A different future was possible. His confinement in a prison cell until his dying breath could quite well be his reality forever. He may never leave. His final days could be spent alone, surrounded only by other prisoners. That fate is not mine.

At work, people his age surround me, living their lives, making choices, shaping their futures. It's impossible not to wonder what my father's life could have been. But dwelling on his mistakes does nothing to change them.

The power to rewrite this story lies within. Strife and restriction are options, and so is triumphing over trauma to claim true freedom. My parents may never acknowledge or support me, but that doesn't change the fact that their legacy continues through me. What they failed to give, life has taught me to seek out and claim for myself. Gratitude fills the heart because the person I am today exists because of all these experiences.

And that's exactly what's happening. Through relentless resilience, life builds on my own terms.

I.N.K. Framework

Instinct: Honor your gut feelings about relationships. Establish clear boundaries with those who cause harm. Stand your ground, when necessary, as I did in my grandparents' home against those who wanted me gone.

Navigation: Focus on what you can control, not what you can't change. Find appropriate support systems like therapy to chart a healthier path. Develop specific strategies to redirect when triggered by old patterns. Accept the reality of difficult situations while actively seeking better alternatives. Remember that sometimes the best navigation involves walking away.

Killer Mindset: Use your painful experiences as lessons, not life sentences. View challenges as opportunities to create a different outcome than those before you. Identify and name your inner critic to diminish its power. Choose to build your life on your own terms despite lack of parental support.

P.E.A.R.L.S. Strategy

Setting boundaries with my parents was the first lesson in what would later become the foundation of my P.E.A.R.L.S. strategy, particularly in claiming sovereignty over my own narrative. Through this painful journey of parental detachment came understanding of the power of strategic positioning, the necessity of adapting to painful realities, and how resilience must be paired with proper rewards to sustain the long path toward freedom.

BREAKING CHAINS
From Silenced Daughter to Sovereign CEO

Male power dynamics in the Latino traditional family were ingrained in my upbringing so much so that I was, and continue to be, invisible as a woman, especially when it comes to my family. Let me get this straight, my family loves me, but my needs and wants are invisible. Not because they aren't important to me or them, but because they simply don't know how to love me differently. The focus continues to be from a man's perspective, where I am obsolete. This seems drastic, and it is, so let me break it down. I had no idea what machismo was during my elementary school years, but when I was in my teenage years, I began to realize the true meaning of machismo and how it affected me. By definition, MACHISMO is an exaggerated or exhilarating sense of power or strength, where the power or strength is given to men and many Latina women not only obey it, but live by it. Ask any woman how machismo has affected their lives and they will have stories for days. Pull out the charcuterie board and your favorite wine, with a side of Kleenex. I recognize that we live in a world where men are more respected than women so the same is true for many women around the world.

As a kid, as early as I could remember, I was in survival mode. I witnessed my mother's abuse. Weekend nights were the worst. These are the days I wish my brain could make my memories travel to a black hole to never return. These days are the most vivid because they caused me the most fear. We, my brother, my mom, and later my 4 sisters and one brother, lived in a one-bedroom apartment in Passaic, NJ, an urban city inhabited with many minorities. My father didn't live with us because he was either in jail, at the local bar drinking or with his mistress(es). When I'd go to bed, I'd awaken to the pounding of the door where my father was yelling for one of us to come and open the door. When we did, we knew we were in for a long night because he would sit in the kitchen with a friend to drink, listen to music and later find a way to mistreat my mom. These are some of the most disgusting memories of my childhood and they deserve to be kept in the past. However, these are the days that taught me to stay quiet, be on alert, my needs and wants did not matter, not to trust men mostly but people in general too, and to always expect something bad to happen.

My uncle, Paciano, who passed while writing this book, came to NJ when I was a little kid, maybe a toddler; he was the only family member from my mother's side to come visit her.   I recall the happiness and joy because he came bearing toys and candy. He was like Santa Claus and we were so excited to have him with us for the day. We played with our toys and enjoyed our candy. As all things are temporary, that happiness was short-lived because that night, my father came home, grabbed a kitchen knife and threatened to kill my mother in her bedroom. To paint the picture, my brother & I slept in the living room that we used as a kid's bedroom and my mother was in the one bedroom with the door closed, but we could hear what was going on. My brother and I wept in silence not knowing if our mother would live another day, but we knew if we said anything, he would definitely do something to her, so we said nothing even though we were dying inside of fear. My father kept saying I know there was another man here with you and she said yes, it was my brother who came to visit. I have no idea how this ended, nor how long this tortuous episode lasted but eventually it ended. We all survived to live another day. However, this experience has lived in my memories with me every day.

Another episode straight out of a horror film was when my mom was ironing clothing and for whatever reason he didn't like how she ironed the clothes so he furiously grabbed the iron to chase me and my mother down the hallway of our apartment building. I ran to my grandmother's house that lived on the same floor in apartment 15 from apartment 17. I don't know how I didn't bring down the door because I was so afraid of being burned by the iron that I hit the door endlessly so that my grandparents could open the door and save us from this monster. I already had a burn on my left arm from the time I had passed by and touched the hot iron with my forearm, so I knew the excruciating pain. I still have that scar on my left arm. I had not even looked at it until the writing of this story. The truth was that my father had no qualms of hurting my mother, so I knew I had to hit that door, yell and scream until the door opened. The crazy part of this is that not one neighbor ever opened their door. I didn't knock on their doors, but I am sure they heard us. Either way, thankfully my grandmother opened the door and was almost bothered, shocked and wondering why we were making all that raucous. The one thing I will never forget was the question she asked me. She asked, what did YOU do to him to get him this upset? Now, thinking back, there was nerve in that question. There is disbelief. There is invisibility again. My fear went unnoticed. My heart is uncared for. My voice is unspoken. My innocence turned into pure villainy. Machismo wins again. Misogyny makes its first appearance.

My father was never one to admit his wrongs, nor take accountability, nor say he was sorry. The one thing he was good at was avoiding responsibility, especially the day he said I wasn't his daughter. Why did he say that? The day he said it, there was a major argument between my father and his parents, my grandparents. I was in my grandparents' living room, which was my customary happy place, until I heard him utter the words, Mimi, my nickname, she isn't my daughter. Until this day, I wonder if he just said that to avoid helping my mother or was it actually true. I still don't know and won't ask anything or anyone because I don't want to know. Thankfully, my uncle Lupe, called me into the kitchen while I was crying about what I had just heard, and he consoled me. I can still recall the tears in his eyes because he knew how devastated I was. I am the first-born. I am unloved by my own father. Who does this?

One thing to take into account here is that my mom was 15 and my dad was 18 when they had me. They were both immature. The change from living in Mexico to now living as immigrants in the United States met my young parents with challenges, struggle and a host of unknowns. I am not making excuses, but I do want to consider their circumstances. I was a little girl. When we came from Mexico, we lived with my grandparents, but at this time, my grandparents had given us our own apartment. My father would not pay his portion; my mom wasn't working so my grandparents had to fit the bill. And I had to live with the fact that my father would not acknowledge me as his daughter. He never apologized. He never brought it up and neither have I. That was the beginning of the end for my father-daughter relationship, which is non-existent. I have long accepted that he was never my father. Thankfully, my grandfather filled that role until his last breath. How I miss Don Porfirio Simón. My grandfather taught me to be fearless when he had the courage to take me on my first car drive. He would say go for it, go for it in Spanish, sin miedo, hijita (without fear). Every time, I am scared, I repeat that in my head and go for it anyway. He was there for me until he fell ill and returned back home to Mexico to a better environment so he could live a longer life. He would always be so happy to see me; I was his first granddaughter. When I traveled with him, people thought I was his daughter, but he would proudly correct them with the fact that she is the daughter of his first-born son.

As an older girl, not yet a teenager, I questioned everything because everything seemed so one-sided. Horrible adults were always telling me what I could do, what I could not do, how I should look, and who I could hang out with. I would say this is normal, regular growing pains, but I had recurring incidents that kept me asking why me? By this time, my mom was raising my brother and two younger sisters alone without the help of my father. My father only came to see my mom for his casual fix, which was either a physical fight or consensual and sometimes not consensual relations. As the oldest, I recall my mother suffering from my father's abuse and the loss of my little sister Catherine who only lived a short 30 days.

Interestingly, I knew she would not live a long life. One day I was jumping on my mom's bed, not realizing my little sister Catherine was on the bed. I only noticed, when I almost jumped on her, but I missed. All I remember was thinking, oh she will only be here temporarily with us and I stopped jumping, got off the bed quickly happy I had not jumped on her and she kept sleeping. Soon thereafter, my mom rushed her for the second time to the hospital where she passed away on my brother's 10th birthday, which was also 4 days short of my 12th birthday. We were so sad when my mom came home alone devastated. I can't imagine what that felt like for her. I recall not having too many emotions. Showing my emotions wasn't commonplace. In fact, not paying my little sister any mind came in handy because being strong for my mom and my siblings, helped me support them by carrying my sister's infant casket with her small corpse to the cemetery because my mother couldn't get herself to do it. I was in the black car alone with her carcass and the driver as a child. I was not even a teenager. Where the hell were the other adults in this? Too busy thinking that this child was not my father's since that was the only story my father knew to tell to keep the misogyny alive and well. It felt as if almost every member of his family disliked my mom or just didn't say anything at least that I could see and that grew over the years. Even my mother sided with my father instead of her own children. She claimed it was to keep us safe from him, and it could be true, but it felt wrong, dismissive, and I was invisible every single time. No matter the angst, who he hurt, the lies he told, the winner of all battles was always the sperm donor, my father.

I always wondered why my father never lived with us, but he never did. He had a childhood that I don't know much about, but do know he was sent to live away from his family. Unfortunately, my father still sits in prison today for a sentence of over 30 years for a crime he committed. When I want to remember what he looks like, I pull up his prison profile to see his picture. Sad, isn't it? But it is our reality. It makes me so sad to know that he has lived almost his entire adult life incarcerated. It is truly unfair that he lived this type of life. I am not fond of him nor want to make excuses for his wrongdoing, but I know he is a person who did what he knew as best as he could, and it led him down this path. At the time of his last arrest, he was staying with my grandparents because he was no longer living with his mistress. As coincidence would have it, I was there too, with my three kids all under 3 years old, after leaving my apartment. I kept thinking of the safety of my children. I knew what he was capable of. I recalled he had slapped me not too long ago while pregnant with my third child after he said, "Look at you, who are you to talk? I replied, "Yes, I found an asshole like you!" To that end, he smacked me right across my face.

I left my own apartment to get away from their father and now I had to face my own father. I could not go to work or go to sleep knowing he was in the other room in the same space as my kids and not too far from my siblings and mom. One night my fear overtook my body and emotions, so I wept and did the only thing I knew I could do, which was to pray to God to take away this fear. The

70

very next day he never came back. He ended up in prison where hopefully he won't die there, but only time will tell what his final fate is. To be clear, I didn't wish him any ill. I just wanted to be safe and give that same safety to my family.

I made the huge mistake of sharing my prayer with a family member because I was shocked how the day after I prayed for safety, my father went to jail. This person had no business sharing and no idea what I lived through, but went back and informed my grandmother who became so angry with me. She had been protecting her son from himself all these years. It wasn't me that sent him to jail; he committed a crime that had consequences so big he couldn't be freed. There was no money that could save him this time. This was not his first time, so the sentence was a long one. My relationship with my grandmother changed forever after that incident. The misogyny is real.

I.N.K. Framework

Instinct: Your gut feelings aren't coincidences; they're your survival mechanism. When I sensed danger from my father or felt my sister wouldn't live long, I was tuning into an innate knowing we all possess. Trust that voice inside you, it knows more than you realize.

Navigation: The world isn't designed for your safety or success. I learned early to read rooms, anticipate foul play, and move through spaces to minimize harm. Map your environment before trying to change it.

Killer Mindset: Being invisible gave me power. I observed everything while being seen as nothing. Your most challenging moments aren't your weakness; they're the source of your unmatched perspective and strength. Own your space unapologetically.

P.E.A.R.L.S. Strategy

The machismo culture that silenced me as a child would later inform crucial elements of my P.E.A.R.L.S. strategy, particularly in understanding how to position myself in environments designed to overlook women's voices. My journey from invisible daughter to vocal leader taught me that execution and leverage are powerful counterforces to systematic erasure, while sovereignty, the ability to define success on my own terms, becomes the ultimate triumph over cultures of silence.

FINDING MY VOICE

From Silence to Influence

Self-protection kept me silent for years. What began as naiveté evolved into deliberate silence after experiencing deception from trusted individuals. The painful lessons taught me to avoid unwanted attention by suppressing my voice, a strategy that served my immediate safety but hindered my long-term growth.

Throughout my youth and early adulthood, inappropriate approaches occurred with disturbing regularity: an older boy in the hallway on my way home, a woman at the printer during my first office job, a man at the airport where I worked, a colleague who repeatedly used "Chicana" as an identifier. Each incident reinforced my instinct to retreat into silence. "I have no choice," I told myself, believing this lie for decades. It's a place I wish no one to ever experience.

The Paradox of a Powerful Voice

The irony wasn't lost on me: physically, my voice carried power that I didn't emotionally own. Family members often referred to me as "la chismosa" (the one who gossips) and requested I lower my volume when excited. This powerful voice could literally startle people from their seats and project across distances, so I was told. During my years working at the airport, it proved valuable when making announcements to stranded passengers during AirTrain disruptions.

Though impactful to others, harnessing this gift remained hidden until my later years. A pivotal moment came when a co-worker in the immigration hall asked what purpose such a distinctive voice would ultimately serve. That question resonated deeply, planting a seed that would take decades to fully bloom.

Music and singing always held appeal for me, yet I couldn't reconcile my natural expressiveness with the message I'd internalized: be quiet, take up less space. Finding my authentic expression required peeling away layers of suppression, a process spanning decades but proving entirely worthwhile.

Early Career: Learning to Speak Through Expertise (1998-2010)

My early professional experiences in the transportation industry revealed my lack of expertise in body language, approachability, and confident speaking. Customer service at the airport brought anxiety and uncertainty about passenger interactions. Standing before hundreds, meeting thousands for the first time, I often felt intimidated by the responsibility to engage verbally.

My supervisors recognized potential I couldn't yet see, encouraging me to use my voice despite my discomfort. With each shift on the AirTrain platforms, my confidence grew incrementally. What began as forced communication gradually evolved into a natural flow where passengers responded positively, sometimes with hugs or appreciation letters. These moments, which I came to call "glimpses of joy," allowed me to see beyond my years of invisibility and trauma.

During this decade, I discovered that knowledge could become my voice when my actual voice felt too risky to use. I focused on learning everything possible about my role, the organization, and the industry. Early career lessons revealed that consistency and expertise meant possessing more information and subject matter knowledge than many others, even those in management positions. Some insecure leaders felt intimidated by this approach, yet this never prevented me from sharing what I knew. When I couldn't trust myself to speak up about personal boundaries, I could at least speak with authority about professional matters.

Professional Evolution: From Individual Contributor to Leader (2010-2020)

In 2010, I transitioned to full-time office work, which meant fewer public interactions but more opportunities to develop my leadership voice. Though I missed the direct contact with passengers, serving employees who served the public brought me deep satisfaction.

The true turning point in my voice development, brand building, and leadership journey came in 2013 when I joined the Hispanic Society, an employee business resource group. Beginning as a member, I quickly advanced to Vice-President and ultimately President. Working alongside a committed partner amplified our impact, bringing remarkable visibility to the organization. During this period, leadership recognition increased as others began noticing the value I contributed.

My service consistently focused on helping others succeed and belong, a mission that felt safer than advocating for myself. Almost imperceptibly, my influence grew to where my opinions and contributions held significance. The strategy I developed was simple but effective: speak up consistently and execute every new idea flawlessly. My guiding principle became "never over-promise and under-deliver, do the opposite."

By 2018, I recognized that appropriate transition timing would prove instrumental for continued growth. One of my most valuable contributions, both personally and for the organization, was the passing of leadership responsibilities to emerging leaders rather than clinging to positions of influence. This seemingly counterintuitive move actually expanded my impact.

Post-Hispanic Society involvement meant continued volunteering with various employee groups. Being recognized as a reliable resource naturally attracted opportunities, including problem-solving requests that might not have come my way through traditional channels. Sharing ideas with appropriate individuals catalyzed unexpected professional advancement. Transforming a beloved profession through strategic influence became my career's crowning achievement during this decade.

Creating New Pathways (2020-Present)

When a new administrative professionals employee group formed in 2020, I saw an opportunity to create something that hadn't existed before. Though I didn't hold senior leadership status, I recognized my potential to make instrumental contributions during their establishment. This realization led to creating a Senior

Advisor role the first and only of its kind in the organization. Remaining silent about my potential contributions seemed pointless when deserved credit for their success was at stake.

Self-advocacy never came easily to me, but by this point in my journey, meeting each moment with presence had become my guiding principle. Later that year, a senior leader asked a question that crystallized my progress: "Why haven't you assumed presentation responsibilities given your significant work contribution?" Until that moment, supporting roles had been my norm. The realization dawned that independent leadership was not just possible but natural. My voice could and should stand alone.

I learned an essential truth: when professional momentum builds, retreating to safety becomes counterproductive. The neighborhood experiences of my childhood with challenging individuals had provided an unexpected perspective on professional situations. I recognized that many people fail to acknowledge their worth, operating at a disadvantage by overlooking proven strategies and lacking the courage to consistently show up, speak authentically, and advocate for others.

Meeting Myself: The Journey Inward

Despite my growing professional influence, a profound lesson awaited me. While giving everything possible to my career and family, people still requested, "Miriam, we need more." An organizational restructuring in 2023 initially seemed devastating but ultimately created space for unprecedented growth. Questions about my future direction emerged as the odds against reaching senior executive levels loomed large, prompting deeper self-reflection than I'd ever undertaken.

One particularly challenging day ended with tears on my train ride home. Facing obstacles directly meant seeing fear as face-everything-and-rise rather than forget-everything-and-run. Feelings of hurt, rejection, and marginalization surfaced intensely. Eventually, my perspective transformed: this difficulty wasn't happening to me as punishment but for me as a catalyst for personal growth.

Memories of a well-connected former executive with media presence and active LinkedIn engagement sparked a realization: personal narratives belong to their owners. My story wouldn't, couldn't end with organizational setbacks. Discovering Adriana Rosales, a Latina committed to publishing one million Latinas, presented an unexpected opportunity. Her invitation focused on leaving a legacy through an anthology series the perfect chance to share my personal experiences. That tearful train ride coincided with receiving the final call email from Adriana. My heartfelt writing led to inclusion in the Latinas 100 anthology!

Advocating for a coaching program followed, having experienced elevation through a coach who encouraged authentic workplace presence, passionate, energetic, devoted to family and being of service. Throughout the coaching process, I recognized that the missing voice had always been my internal one. Until that point, most of my actions served others, but this marked a personal season of growth.

At 43, despite an impactful position, financial stability, a loving peaceful marriage, and children progressing toward independence, isolation persisted. My entire existence had centered around others, from childhood caring for my mother's emotional needs, siblings, and cousins, to becoming a mother at 18. Caretaking had been mastered, but self-knowledge was completely out of touch for myself. A career built on serving others brought fulfillment, but solitude remained unfamiliar territory. Questions arose: What next? With no friends to call, no children needing attention, a working spouse, and family members pursuing their paths, my daughter Rosa's words echoed with profound truth: "Mom, have you ever met you?" This question resonated because self-knowledge had been sacrificed for others' needs.

My adult children showed diminishing interest in companionship, while my spouse's opposite work schedule limited quality time to brief evening interactions and weekends. My beautiful home filled with accomplishments still felt empty without a deeper connection to myself.

Reflection permeated my mind, heart, and body during this period of introspection. Gratitude for achievements, connections, helping others, beautiful and intelligent children, and a supportive spouse mingled with emerging questions about personal identity and aspirations beyond professional success.

Unexpected thoughts surfaced, including asking my spouse about having children after several years of marriage though this possibility remained closed since my partner never wanted children unless able to provide full-time care. Independence remained her priority, a choice deserving my respect. Dreams of experiencing pregnancy with a loving partner remained unfulfilled. However, the gift of having a partner who loved my existing children as their own proved infinitely more valuable. My compromise came in the form of a Yorkshire Terrier puppy Miko, five pounds of lovable energy with yellow, my new favorite color.

Finding My Authentic Voice

Throughout my life, my voice had created significant ripples pursuing education, recognizing love at first sight (even after picking-up my future wife from her then-boyfriend's house), and seeking career advancement that transformed my trajectory. However, these happened during constant motion without the stillness needed for genuine self-listening.

Through introspective work with transformative coaches in 2023-2024, I met both my inner critic "Jackie" (my parents' almost-chosen name for me) and my authentic voice "Sunny." Jackie constantly questioned: What if that alternative identity had been chosen for me? Perhaps maternal acceptance and paternal love comparable to that shown to another daughter named Jacqueline might have followed. Sunny, however, spoke the truth: I am exactly who I'm meant to be, shaped by every experience into someone with unique wisdom to share.

This self-discovery brought interesting revelations. Opening to vulnerability represented the greatest challenge I ever faced. Transforming trauma into wisdom brought deep satisfaction. Being seemingly sidelined ultimately created different opportunities to shine. As one path closed, another revealed itself. Learning to listen to internal wisdom, share authentically, and remain present became my new foundation.

During one particularly powerful coaching session, I found myself approaching questions mechanically until disrupted by the group coach. My emotional composure faltered as the realization hit: merely checking boxes rather than being fully present had become my pattern. That marked the final instance of half-hearted engagement. Since then, my transformation has been complete, fully committed rather than partially invested. Connection has grown exponentially, as has the ability to hear that authentic inner voice.

My journey with "Sunny" continues with mutual contentment. Perhaps the most gratifying aspect of becoming an author? When the publisher used the term "superstar" as my identification external validation of an internal truth I'd finally embraced.

Looking back on my journey beyond silence, I now understand that my leadership voice was forged in the very crucible of trauma that once threatened to extinguish it. Those early experiences of exploitation, loss, and invisibility didn't diminish my power; they became the foundation upon which I built it. The moments where my voice was suppressed became my motivation to ensure others could be heard. My encounters with those who wielded power inappropriately taught me to recognize and cultivate authentic influence. Even my inner critic "Jackie" has become an ally, reminding me of how far I've traveled from that defenseless child to the executive who creates spaces where others can thrive.

My scars truly have become stars, not just illuminating my own path but casting light so others might find their way forward as well. The transformation from silence to leadership wasn't just about finding my voice, it was about discovering that my voice, shaped by every painful experience and triumph, was exactly what the world needed to hear.

I.N.K. Framework

Instinct: Trust your inner wisdom when processing trauma and finding your voice. My journey taught me that my deep feeling and thinking nature initially made me vulnerable to exploitation, yet these same qualities eventually became my greatest strengths in leadership. Learning to distinguish between vulnerability that harms and vulnerability that heals required trusting my gut about when, where, and with whom to share my experiences. The question isn't whether to trust your instincts, but how to refine them through experience.

Navigation: Map your path through the terrain from silence to influence. I moved from complete silence about my experiences to strategic disclosure that served both my healing and my leadership development. By acknowledging past experiences without letting them control my present, I created a route toward authentic expression that honored both my pain and my power to transcend it. Effective navigation means understanding when to speak, when to listen, and how to create new pathways where none existed before.

Killer Mindset: Transform what wounded you into what strengthens your voice. Rather than staying frozen in victimhood or silence, I chose to use my experiences as catalysts for developing a powerful leadership voice. This mindset shift allowed me to see that my most painful moments of silencing could become the very foundation for a voice that helps others find theirs. Your most challenging experiences aren't liabilities, they're the unique perspective that only you can bring to leadership conversations.

P.E.A.R.L.S. Strategy

My journey from silence to influence embodies the P.E.A.R.L.S. strategy in action. I strategically Positioned myself where my expertise could have an impact, from joining the Hispanic Society to creating the Senior Advisor role. Through consistent Execution of my "never over-promise, over-deliver" principle, I built trust in my voice among colleagues and leaders. I demonstrated adaptability by evolving from expertise-based authority to authentic leadership as circumstances changed, finding new channels like writing when traditional paths closed. Resilience developed through transforming each attempt to silence me into greater determination to be heard. Ultimately, I achieved sovereignty by owning my narrative and defining authentic expression on my terms, recognizing that my right to speak comes from within rather than external validation.

DRIVE IN THE EMERGENCY LANE
Charting Your Own Path

Every professional journey has its own unmarked territory. The path to success often requires navigating beyond conventional routes, finding the emergency lanes when traffic stands still. This chapter explores how ambitious professionals can break through gatekeeping systems, craft unique career trajectories, and transform personal challenges into strategic advantages. Rather than accepting predetermined paths, true innovation comes from honoring instincts, mapping deliberate navigation strategies, and developing a mindset that turns obstacles into opportunities. For those who have felt marginalized or underestimated, these pages reveal practical frameworks for leveraging distinctive perspectives as competitive advantages in corporate environments. Through real examples and actionable strategies, you will discover how to remain authentic while strategically positioning yourselves for unprecedented growth, breaking patterns that no longer serve, and creating roles that showcase your unique talents and vision.

From Assimilation to Belonging

Assimilation is what many were taught to do to fit in. Here is where they say make lemonade out of lemons because this is what you get. The challenge is to confront assimilation and demonstrate a new approach, a new method with what each person brings. Inclusion is the opposite of assimilation which is a term that's not that new but increasingly applied in workplace settings. Belonging takes it to the Big Screen because here is where a person can thrive with their own perspective, their special sauce. Every person has such richness to them that every mind is a different world. People bring the unique experience of their lives, the lens from which they see and the core values with which they navigate their behaviors and their actions.

In elementary school years, reading about the need for immigrants to assimilate to another country sparked questions. For many like me, this concept made no sense, igniting the rebel within and lighting an advocacy flame that burned deep.

Thankfully, through many experiences shared within this chapter, instead of assimilating, the path has been to create spaces for the reinvention of what leadership looks like. The redefinition of what a person from certain backgrounds should be doing. So much so that when meeting the honorable Dolores Huerta at the Hispanic Leadership Summit at the United Nations on December 6, 2023, a special moment occurred. I had no idea she would be there. I went to get information about the latest statistics on the Latino journey to take back with me. But, I did a double take when I realized I was in the same room as Dolores Huerta - the Dolores Huerta. During a break, I saw her go to the center of the floor where she then exited. Not sure what made me get up to get closer to her incoming pathway to approach her. There was this overwhelming knowing that I just had to speak to her. I waited for her to enter the center of the floor. So did someone else who jumped right in and began speaking to her. I approached her slowly, waiting for their interaction to finish, but without hesitation, Dolores stopped looking at the person speaking to her. She turned to me. Looked at me. Saw me. Extended her arms towards me to invite me into her space. After a brief introduction, she whispered the most amazing words I'll never forget. It was exactly what I needed to hear. She said, "You are what we call a Chingona."

Assimilation reared its ugly head several times and began early in elementary school. The bilingual class is where it all first started. Children with parents who didn't speak English were often placed in bilingual classes. The negative energy from being in a bilingual class quickly taught that these classes were for kids considered less intelligent. Assumptions were made that children didn't speak English because their parents didn't, and therefore, their place was in the bilingual class. Administrations would mention if students showed signs of learning English quickly, then they'd consider moving them to a "regular" class. This proved incorrect for many students who were moved when teachers quickly noticed they should not have been in those classrooms to begin with. Evaluations would reveal intelligence, contradicting the notion that speaking Spanish translated to being less capable. The message received was that assimilating to learning and speaking the language of the U.S. would lead to thriving. Obviously, this isn't true because speaking two languages means something altogether more significant. Navigating two cultural norms brings flexibility and adaptability. Neither culture is better than the other, but both are different. Too bad proving English proficiency was what some thought would make a person more intelligent. They were wrong.

Proving belonging happened to many at the border after visiting Mexico. Customs agents asked me several questions to prove my status in the U.S. Understanding this concept of proving belonging sometimes makes people think they don't belong. Don't let the way systems work question your ability and worth.

The Next Level: Be A Gate Breaker

Gatekeeping is another term for an unspoken practice. There's criteria to meet, magic potions to stir up that quite possibly only a few are privileged to hold the recipe for that have been passed down and become hurdles too high to jump over. Those who manage to get to the decision tables need to obtain the codes, define the codes, and rewrite the codes. The more people do differently than those before them, the easier it'll get for others when trying to join these groups. The challenge offered to everyone is the million-dollar question: Am I a gatekeeper? Am I deliberately holding people back? Is what was done before still the best way forward, especially in who and how we do our work? Am I only allowing a specific person who fits an antiquated mold to get through to the next level? If you answer yes, you are a gatekeeper. We have come so far and have broken cycles. Now it's time to go to the next level. Be someone who welcomes new ways of doing the ordinary so we can collectively become extraordinary. For those doing the work...we see you and we are so proud of you. We are the ones going the extra mile and going before anyone else. We are creating new spaces, showing the way first. It is a difficult mission to take on but if you do it and others do it, the possibilities are endless. More will join the Leaders of Leaders Community; we have begun a movement. A movement to tackle the same spaces where we are no longer outnumbered but empowered.

I.N.K. Framework

Instinct: Honor your inner compass when navigating professional crossroads. In a world that demands assimilation, your unique perspective serves as an invaluable guide. When systems try to classify and limit your potential, like being placed in a "bilingual class" that carries unwarranted assumptions, trust the internal voice that recognizes your true capabilities. Your instincts often perceive opportunities and pathways invisible to conventional wisdom.

Navigation: Chart your own path beyond established routes. Like approaching Dolores Huerta with the intuitive knowing that connection was essential, strategic navigation means positioning yourself at the intersection of preparation and opportunity. Map the professional landscape not just to understand existing structures, but to identify the unmarked territories where your distinctive talents can create unprecedented value.

Killer Mindset: Refuse to accept limitations others place on you. When systems attempt to define your capabilities, like assuming language barriers equate to intelligence, maintain unwavering determination in your own worth. The experience of proving belonging at borders or in boardrooms builds the resilience to view rejection as redirection. Transform the bilingualism of language, culture, and experience into your "special sauce" that enables you to break patterns, challenge gatekeeping, and consistently perform at the level of your vision rather than others' expectations.

P.E.A.R.L.S. Strategy

The P.E.A.R.L.S. strategy equates to emerging from emergency where true innovators drive, positioning yourself as a gate-breaker who builds a distinctive brand that commands attention before you speak, executing consistently above expectations while refusing to assimilate to outdated norms, adapting strategically without abandoning your destination when systems try to classify and limit your potential, building resilience by transforming border-crossing experiences into professional strength and celebrating being called a "Chingona," leveraging every relationship and connection like Dolores Huerta's recognition to accelerate your growth, and ultimately claiming sovereignty by creating spaces for the reinvention of what leadership looks like rather than waiting for permission to lead. This polished yet unfiltered approach transforms the bilingualism of language, culture, and lived experience into your competitive edge, your "special sauce," allowing you to play chess while others play checkers, carving out space in a professional landscape that wasn't designed for you without losing the authentic perspective that makes you extraordinary and building a community of "Leaders of Leaders" who collectively break cycles and redefine excellence.

CHARTING AN UNSTOPPABLE PATH

The Canvas of Your Career

Think about your life like a blank canvas where each day can start with a different color as the base. As you determine your intention, you choose which elements to add, remove, or modify. When you tap into your experiences with intention, innovation emerges. This is especially powerful when surrounded by people who inspire and challenge you.

Careers follow similar patterns of growth and transformation. Like garden peonies that grow taller and produce more blooms each spring, professional development builds upon itself. We begin as novices with what others might perceive as limited experience, but with each working day, competencies stack in our knowledge bank. The people we encounter in organizations teach us invaluable lessons about business, culture, and strategic direction.

The trajectory of your career isn't predetermined; it's created through deliberate choices and consistent action. While a title may be assigned based on experience and accomplishments, what you make of that role remains entirely at your discretion. Job crafting, actively reshaping your position to align with your strengths and values, opens opportunities and makes work more fulfilling. Although some believe there is no flexibility within organizational structures, I've discovered that influence and creativity can transform any role when approached strategically.

Even positions that appear to have limited systematic influence can become platforms for significant impact when you focus on improving experiences, fulfilling needs, and building credibility. Leadership emerges not just through formal authority but through intention deliberately building your brand and gaining trust to create momentum.

The Power of Taking the Path Less Traveled (1990s)

Being part of the in-crowd has never been my preference, not in school, not in my career. Choosing the less traveled path created unique opportunities: graduating in the top percentiles while raising three children, completing my degree with honors as a full-time working parent, navigating complex relationships, managing promotions across multiple states, and eventually creating roles that didn't previously exist.

This journey required learning to trust and take risks, sometimes against my instincts. For someone whose safety had been compromised through betrayal and trauma, accepting opportunities often felt counterintuitive rather than natural. Therapy became essential in unlearning the ways past experiences distorted my thinking about possibilities.

The process demanded checking thoughts against reality and building resilience, developing the emotional muscles to withstand change and uncertainty. Understanding that some people genuinely have your best interests at heart takes time when your experience suggests otherwise. Though reaching this empowered state might require decades of intentional work, the growth continues throughout life.

For many with backgrounds similar to mine, constant forward motion becomes necessary because there simply isn't another option. Looking back at my achievements reveals a pattern of working in what I call "the emergency lane," taking unconventional paths that sometimes meant moving at an accelerated pace, sometimes meant seeking urgent assistance, and sometimes meant facing serious consequences for bold choices.

My Unconventional Career Trajectory (1998-2010)

My earliest leadership opportunities emerged during high school, when teachers recognized my aptitude for numbers, business, and organization. Their encouragement led to participation in the Peer Leadership Program and Future Business Leaders of America, where I facilitated groups helping freshmen transition to high school. These formative experiences taught me to lead teams, complete projects, and build community skills that would become foundational to my professional development.

My first job came unexpectedly at 16, when a mall store manager spotted me while shopping with my grandparents. Working at that science store provided crucial experiences in creative merchandising, customer service, and potential leadership. Being entrusted with designing displays according to my vision built early confidence. The store managers recognized potential beyond my years, involving me in store openings and discussing future management opportunities.

The pivotal career shift came after high school graduation. My aunt Gloria, recognizing my need to fund college and my untapped potential, convinced me to interview at the local airport. This opportunity arrived at a critical moment when I needed to establish independence. Her practical support extended to helping me acquire transportation, which research shows is crucial for accessing better employment outside disadvantaged communities. This step marked my departure from familiar territory into new professional landscapes.

The airport interview presented a moment of identity assertion. My aunt advised me against wearing my signature black eyeliner and dark lipstick, suggesting it looked too "chola." Though I heard her concern, I remained authentic to my personal style a decision I've maintained throughout my career, as evidenced by my book cover photo. The long wait for the interview tested my determination, but securing that position, making decent wages directly out of high school, transformed my trajectory. I remain grateful to every manager who saw past my socioeconomic background to recognize my potential.

Building Versatility Through Diverse Experience (1998-2012)

This airport position introduced me to complex organizational systems: union operations, manual processes before automation, and hybrid positions that built versatile skills across customer service and administration. Becoming the only full-time person in my specialized role meant carving a unique path defined by my particular skills and contributions.

Working in this environment for years without a college degree provided me invaluable experience in operations, office management, and specialized knowledge. Though colleagues called me a "jack of all trades" capable of handling diverse responsibilities, advancement to management remained difficult for me to get into. This limitation led to strategic patience waiting for better opportunities while continuing to build my capabilities.

What I initially perceived as setbacks often revealed themselves as redirections toward better paths. When my managers unexpectedly called me to serious meetings, my first reaction was concern: Had I done something wrong? Why would they suggest I look elsewhere? Only later did I understand they were selflessly directing me toward greater opportunities, seeing possibilities for my growth that my current position couldn't provide. Their willingness to let go of a valuable team member demonstrated extraordinary professional support.

Strategic Career Navigation (2013-Present)

Creating my first professional resume after a decade and engaging with formal application processes marked another transition. When multiple job offers arrived simultaneously, I faced a critical decision point. Rather than taking the supervisory role with slightly higher pay, I strategically chose the entry-level position in a department with greater long-term advancement potential.

This decision reflected my understanding that career development isn't about immediate gains but long-term trajectory. Taking the lower-level position created opportunities for multiple promotions and salary increases over time, whereas the supervisory role would have placed me in a smaller department with limited growth potential. This foresight proved correct when I quickly gained out-of-title responsibilities and compensation when a colleague took medical leave just eight months after I started.

The subsequent years demonstrated the power of strategic career planning. I completed my college degree, earned professional certifications, received multiple promotions, became a certified coach, won a corporate achievement award, and quadrupled my initial salary. My five-year goal to double my income was far exceeded through compounding opportunities and strategic positioning.

Simultaneously, I built influence through volunteer leadership with employee resource groups, progressing from member to secretary, vice president, and eventually president. This parallel path led to creating the first Senior Advisor role and establishing development programs that have benefited hundreds of colleagues. This year alone, we celebrated 111 employees completing our development program and established 9 additional Senior Advisor positions across all employee resource groups.

My commitment to creating opportunities for others stems from profound gratitude to my friend who saved my life, my grandparents and family who supported my upbringing, and even my parents whose sacrifices contributed to my success despite our difficult relationship. This obligation extends to my children, community, and future generations who deserve pathways to achievement and fulfillment.

I.N.K. Framework

Instinct: Honor your intuition even when it conflicts with conventional wisdom such as my decision to remain authentic to my personal style during interviews and throughout my career opened doors to environments where I could thrive as my genuine self rather than someone's expectation.

Navigation: Identify the difference between short-term gains and long-term trajectory. For example, my strategic choice to take an entry-level position with greater advancement potential rather than an immediate supervisory role created opportunities for multiple promotions and exponential salary growth.

Killer Mindset: Transform perceived limitations into unique advantages, without a college degree early in my career, I built irreplaceable operational expertise and specialized knowledge that made me invaluable in ways formal education couldn't replicate.

P.E.A.R.L.S. Strategy

Your unique experiences, including your struggles, have equipped you with perspectives and capabilities others may not possess. Examine where you're currently applying your energy and ask whether it's creating the long-term impact you desire. Consider what "job crafting" opportunities exist in your current role to align your daily activities with your strengths and values. Remember that sovereignty isn't granted, it's claimed through consistent excellence, strategic positioning, and the courage to create space for your authentic leadership.

STRATEGIES FOR PROFESSIONAL GROWTH

Map Your Journey with Precision

Begin by assessing your current position within your career landscape. Without awareness of your starting point, gaps in your preparation, and clear destination, you risk stagnation. Moving forward requires intentionality to determine whether incremental progress or transformative leaps best serve your goals.

Research thoroughly: understand role requirements, compensation patterns, organizational structures, and who currently holds positions you aspire to reach. Study their backgrounds, tenure, and career progression. Rather than focusing solely on your next step, envision roles 3-5 levels ahead, then work backward to identify necessary skills and experiences.

In today's accelerated professional environment, preparing for advanced positions earlier creates competitive advantage. Review your capabilities against senior role requirements, collect position descriptions throughout your organization, and understand how responsibilities evolve across levels. This methodical preparation equips you not only to advance personally but eventually to guide others.

Transform Rejection into Redirection

Career advancement rarely follows a linear path. Multiple interviews, rejections, and redirections typically precede significant breakthroughs. The irony of professional life often places you under the leadership of people who previously declined to hire you. Rather than holding grudges, view these moments as evidence that timing matters more than permanent limitations.

When improvement suggestions meet resistance, practice strategic patience. Let initial refusals pass without discouragement, knowing that sharing your ideas with receptive stakeholders will eventually transform rejection into support. "No" frequently means "not yet" rather than "never."

The visionary perspective you bring may initially be invisible to others. When hired to implement improvements but met with resistance, I recognize that sometimes organizations need additional information, clearer direction, better timing, or different environments before embracing change. Your persistence through these phases distinguishes you as a transformative leader.

Make the Implicit Explicit

Becoming unstoppable requires translating your vision into a language others can understand and support. Since each person perceives the world differently, no one automatically comprehends your goals or intentions. Effective influence requires tailoring communication to your audience's needs and perspective.

When presenting ideas, adjust your message to match your audience's knowledge level and priorities. Be concise yet comprehensive, and avoid overwhelming emails that obscure key points. When you possess greater subject matter expertise than managers, focus on explaining concepts clearly rather than assuming shared understanding.

The art of making implicit knowledge explicit seems straightforward but requires deep self-awareness, audience understanding, and goal clarity. The most sophisticated leadership often appears effortless precisely because the complex work of translation has been handled with such care.

Embody Your Next Role Before You Have It

Your daily performance creates a continuous interview for future opportunities. While you may not see senior leaders regularly, they receive information about your impact and approach. Their responsibility includes identifying future talent and innovation sources, making your consistent excellence visible even when direct observation is limited.

Maintain impeccable standards even when no audience is present, allowing integrity to become habitual rather than performative. Research shows that women often need to demonstrate capabilities in current roles before promotion, while men are frequently hired based on potential. Responding to this reality means consistently performing at the level of your desired position rather than your current one.

Higher-level positions increasingly come through informal channels, the "shoulder tap" for those demonstrating readiness through consistent performance and strategic visibility. While formal interviews remain part of advancement processes, they represent confirmation of observed capability rather than initial discovery.

Break Patterns That Limit Your Potential

The power to become exceptional lies in your willingness to break limiting patterns both those imposed externally and those you've internalized. Rather than focusing on statistical limitations for people with your background characteristics, direct your attention toward those who have succeeded despite similar constraints.

Demographics shift through individual decisions to pursue advancement. Each person who breaks through a barrier increases representation and creates pathways for others. When roles evolve beyond their original descriptions through your contributions, advocate for reclassification that reflects these changes.

Distinguishing between patterns that serve your growth and those that limit it requires ongoing assessment. When identifying restrictive patterns, prepare to break them by deliberately raising your hand when others remain silent, presenting visions when others focus on problems, and creating paths where none previously existed.

For many from marginalized backgrounds, personal challenges become catalysts for extraordinary ambition and determination. The very brokenness that might have limited others becomes fuel for unstoppable progress.

I.N.K. Framework

Instinct: The career breakthroughs I've experienced came from trusting my authentic instincts from maintaining my personal style despite my aunt's well-intended advice to selecting the entry-level position over the supervisory role when conventional wisdom suggested otherwise. Learning to recognize and trust these internal signals allows you to make decisions aligned with your true path rather than following predetermined routes.

Navigation: My professional growth demonstrates the importance of deliberately mapping unconventional trajectories. From creating hybrid positions at the airport to establishing the Senior Advisor role, I've consistently crafted unique paths rather than waiting for established routes to appear. Strategic navigation means understanding not just the organization's current structure but envisioning how your distinctive talents can reshape that structure.

Killer Mindset: The determination to push beyond limitations whether facing rejection, working without a degree, or managing family responsibilities alongside career advancement, defined my approach. This unstoppable attitude transforms obstacles into opportunities for differentiation and innovation. Consistently performing at your desired level rather than your current position prepares you for advancement before formal recognition arrives.

P.E.A.R.L.S. Strategy

My journey from the margins to leadership demonstrates the P.E.A.R.L.S. strategy in action. I strategically positioned myself by building expertise and visibility that made me indispensable, then consistently executed above expectations, turning an entry-level role into a platform for influence. My adaptability was demonstrated through my ability to pivot between customer-facing and administrative responsibilities as organizational needs evolved. Resilience is developed through transforming rejection into redirection while celebrating incremental progress. I leveraged every relationship from my aunt's initial support to mentors who guided my development, multiplying my impact through collaborative advancement.

Finally, achieving sovereignty meant creating entirely new roles and programs rather than waiting for permission to lead, ultimately redefining what leadership could look like for future generations from backgrounds similar to mine.

BEYOND THE SILENCE

How Trauma Shaped My Leadership Voice

"Power over others is weakness disguised as strength. True power is within, and it is available to you now." - Eckhart Tolle

Silence has been both my prison and my sanctuary. Growing up in environments where my voice was often stifled or ignored, I learned early that words could either be weapons used against me or shields I could wield for protection. This journey from imposed silence to deliberate speech has shaped not just my personal narrative, but fundamentally defined my approach to leadership.

The path from trauma to triumph is rarely straightforward. Like many who have weathered childhood adversity, my relationship with power began from a position of powerlessness. The experiences that threatened to break me instead became the foundation upon which I built my resilience. This chapter is not merely a recounting of painful memories, but rather an exploration of how those very moments that could have silenced me permanently instead forged my authentic leadership voice.

What follows is not simply a story of survival, but a roadmap for transformation, showing how wounds, when properly tended, can become wellsprings of wisdom. Through frameworks like I.N.K. and

P.E.A.R.L.S., I've discovered that our deepest vulnerabilities, once acknowledged and integrated, can become our greatest strengths. My journey reveals that true leadership emerges not despite our traumas, but sometimes because of how we've metabolized them into insight and compassion.

In recent years, experts have said to be vulnerable and step out of the shadows of shame. Well, in their context that might work, but in mine, not so much. I've been tired of being vulnerable most of my life. Some of us don't have the same vulnerabilities as others. For some, exposing our vulnerabilities can lead to harm, deception, and even death. The degree to which we show up could make us most vulnerable to experiences we can't come back from. Meaning, that for most of my life I've been a deep feeler and thinker, and this has placed me in situations that made me vulnerable. In retrospect, I knew no other way to be.

Power dynamics play a delicate part in how I've experienced life. In the past, I had typically been on the side of the greater negative power. The positive power was often on the other side of my life's balance sheet. You may ask why? Well, let me share why. The control was mostly driven by others for a long time, but I learned to inch my way to the positive side with a lot of wit and my hunger to learn. The negative side taught me lessons that I carry with me everywhere, and to no surprise, I've gained wisdom that can only come from experience.

For me, one of the worst human experiences is being ridiculed, taken advantage of, and being left alone during my most vulnerable moments. To justify these experiences, people say, look at how strong you are now. Yes, do I have a choice? Either I give into the darkness or get up and move on with my life, seeking the rainbow after the rainstorm. Getting back up is hard, sometimes nearly impossible, and at times shameful, but moving forward was and continues to be the only path up and out. Is it easy? Not really, but can you get through it? Yes, eventually. This type of inner knowing is what has, for the most part, shaped my voice.

Reclaiming Power: Beyond Vulnerability

Looking back, my vulnerability peaked when I was at the mercy of others. These experiences, committed to paper just once, speak of a time I disclosed an event that I experienced during my elementary school years. This experience I speak of, I will not go into detail; just know it happened. The purpose of writing it down on paper was to reassure others with similar experiences that they aren't alone. To absolve that younger self of misplaced blame. To demonstrate that a single moment cannot dictate an entire life narrative. For years, this memory remained locked in a sacred safe, but the time has come to voice this unexplained yet authentic experience and finally release it. Such burdens deserve no permanent residence within anyone. The incident stemmed from someone in authority exploiting a defenseless child. The exact age remains unclear in my memory. Only one person, my spouse, Kerry, knows these details. I entrusted her with this knowledge to foster deeper understanding between us in ways unnecessary for others. My heart goes out to every defenseless child that has ever been exploited and left to fend for themselves.

Nothing more needs articulation beyond acknowledging it happened to me. I accept it as a horrific experience while recognizing it no longer controls my actions, thoughts, or capacity to forgive, and the love inside me marks true liberation. So many stories have shaped me, and I will share some that completely transformed me, in particular what I shared earlier. The death of my friend who saved my life.

My Younger Years

Still, in high school my senior year arrived with promise serving as a peer leader, working at the World of Science, and envisioning college life ahead. The future had always represented an escape from poverty, a focal point of determination and hope. Eternal gratitude extends to those teachers in Passaic, New Jersey, who proved integral in revealing different possibilities for me and my future. These educators recognized my potential beyond my challenging circumstances. For years, circumstances maintained the upper hand, but finally, my ability began shining through. The path toward a brighter future seemed clear until...

I was introduced to a man who appeared through a mutual friend. Initial instincts signaled I should reject him; there were red flags that warranted attention but went unheeded. He crafted lies resembling romantic fairy tales, I easily believed. I was yearning for connection. During the summer following high school graduation, while pursuing business administration studies, my pregnancy due to this entanglement changed everything. My shame prevented me from returning to the university to finish the summer program. His seemingly good intentions evaporated when reality set in. Life suddenly mirrored my mother's experiences. A cycle repeated despite my determination to break free from family inherited traumas. The crushing realization of abandoned dreams weighed on me heavily: college should have been my current reality, not this unexpected detour.

Since childhood, I have sought love in all the wrong places. My grandparents and certain aunts and uncles offered genuine affection, but maternal and paternal love, nonexistent, remained my deepest longing. The absence of real love taught me falsely that love was undeserved, a lesson with decades-long repercussions. Pursuing college proved challenging as motherhood became my priority.

My journey from difficult childhood experiences led directly to complicated adult situations. So many times, I felt I was not in control of my life. Heartaches accumulated to insurmountable levels, requiring decades to acknowledge the pain, mistrust, and pervasive unworthiness. Feeling exploited contradicted others' suggestions that such treatment was somehow invited or deserved. How could anyone request such behavior? For my children's sake, forgiveness has been granted and forward movement achieved, though scars remained as a testament to my journey.

Echoes Into Action: From Silence to Resonance

The child who once sat in fearful silence could never have imagined the leader she would become. Yet here I stand, voice clear, my purpose defined. The journey from victim to victor wasn't accomplished through denial of pain but through its integration into a more complete self. By acknowledging both the darkness and light of my experiences, I've discovered that authentic leadership grows from this wholeness.

My story is simultaneously unique and universal. While the specific circumstances of my trauma differ from others, the process of reclaiming power resonates across human experience. Through the I.N.K. framework, I've learned to trust my instincts, navigate complex situations, and maintain a killer mindset that refuses surrender. The P.E.A.R.L.S. strategy has transformed positional weakness into strategic strength, creating ripples of impact beyond my individual healing.

The voice I've cultivated doesn't speak despite my trauma, it speaks with the depth and authority that only comes from walking through fire and emerging transformed. This voice now reaches out to others navigating their own silences, offering not empty platitudes about resilience, but honest testimony that darkness can indeed give way to dawn. My leadership philosophy emanates from this central truth: our most authentic power emerges when we transform our wounds into wisdom and our silence into speech that resonates with truth.

Your journey may differ from mine, but the invitation remains the same, trust the wisdom your body holds, navigate toward your truth with unwavering determination, and develop the mindset that refuses to be defined by your wounds. In doing so, you too may discover that your voice, once silenced, can become a powerful instrument for change, creating echoes that inspire others to break their own silence and step into their fullest leadership potential.

I.N.K. Framework

Instinct: My journey taught me to trust the inner wisdom my body always knew. When I met the man through my mutual friend, my "initial instincts signaled I should reject him" - so many red flags I unfortunately ignored. This painful lesson strengthened my commitment to honor my gut feelings. Being a "deep feeler and thinker" initially made me vulnerable, but I've learned to transform this sensitivity into an early warning system that protects and guides me through challenging situations.

Navigation: Learning to map my way through trauma required understanding power dynamics and gradually shifting "to the positive side with a lot of wit and my hunger to learn." I navigated from being "at the mercy of others" to reclaiming my own agency. This navigation wasn't straightforward; it meant acknowledging when "circumstances maintained the upper hand" while still finding pathways forward, even when my educational journey was detoured by early motherhood.

Killer Mindset: Refusing to surrender to darkness defined my approach to adversity. When faced with ridicule and exploitation, I recognized "either I give into the darkness or get up and move on with my life, seeking the rainbow after the rainstorm." This resilient mindset didn't come naturally; it was forged through repeatedly choosing to rise despite shame and obstacles. I transformed experiences that could have destroyed me into wisdom that can only come from experience.

P.E.A.R.L.S. Strategy

My journey beyond silence reflects the full spectrum of the P.E.A.R.L.S. strategy. I Positioned myself to grow beyond my circumstances, moving from exploitation to empowerment and recognizing potential despite challenges. My Execution focused on consistently fulfilling responsibilities as a mother while maintaining sight of larger goals, creating a foundation for my leadership approach. Adaptability allowed me to navigate unexpected detours like early pregnancy without abandoning my core determination. Resilience developed through acknowledging that recovery is difficult yet possible, transforming each setback into strength. I Leveraged both positive influences like supportive teachers and negative experiences as catalysts for growth and connection with others. Finally, my Sovereignty emerged through accepting past trauma while refusing to let it control my actions, thoughts, or capacity to forgive creating the true liberation that allowed my authentic leadership voice to emerge.

INK & INSTINCT
The Courage to be Seen

Have you ever felt the urge to shrink away when someone praised your work? Or found yourself unable to celebrate your accomplishments, even as others cheered you on? You're not alone. The journey from dismissing recognition to embracing your true value is one of the most profound transformations on the path to personal sovereignty.

In this chapter, I invite you into one of my most vulnerable spaces, the lifelong struggle to accept praise, recognition, and opportunity with the same grace and openness with which they were offered. For too many years, a "resting bitch face" became my shield against the discomfort of being truly seen, a defensive posture born from childhood experiences where my achievements were either dismissed or undermined.

The truth is, many of us, especially women, people of color, and those raised in cultures that prioritize humility have been conditioned to deflect compliments, minimize our accomplishments, and accept whatever is given to us without question. We've been taught that asking for what we truly want or need is somehow selfish or inappropriate.

But what if rejecting the path others have laid out for you isn't rebellion, it's revelation? What if saying "no, thank you" to opportunities that don't align with your authentic self isn't ungrateful, it's essential to honoring your journey?

As you read through these pages, I'll share how I transformed from someone frozen in the spotlight to someone who can stand in her power and worth. We'll explore how the I.N.K. Framework: Instinct, Navigation, and Killer Mindset, coupled with the P.E.A.R.L.S. Strategy can help you thaw out your frozen state and step fully into the recognition you deserve.

This isn't just about learning to accept compliments with a smile. It's about claiming your right to define success on your own terms and charting a course that honors your unique gifts, even when, especially when, there is no established path to follow.

Are you ready to transform from accepting what others give you to intentionally designing what you want to receive? To move from broken mirrors to polished pearls? Let's begin.

Thaw Out Your Frozen State

Apologies to everyone that has been a great person to me, who has given me an opportunity and who has seen me. Unfortunately, being able to receive recognition, accolades or compliments were not easy for me. In fact, they made me uncomfortable. For about one million reasons and one I could never get myself to see my true value. Whether that was due to my unconscious past traumas or my limited understanding of how wonderful I truly am. I'll never know but that time for me has passed and I've grown and I recognize my full awesomeness now.

Whether I received a promotion, an award, good reviews at work or a kiss, a hug from my kids or a nice gesture from a stranger, all of these experiences led to what is well-known as resting bitch face. People must have asked themselves whether or not I was actually mad at them for giving me something good. It's so unfortunate that something good felt so uncomfortable to me. It's the opposite of what I wanted to do but I was stuck in that state. The emotion was not being mad but my reaction was silent, calm and almost with no emotion. My excitement didn't surface, often feeling as if diving into feeling any real emotion would dismantle my very existence. At least that is how it felt. What if I truly felt what was being gifted to me? What if I felt for real? And I did feel. I felt love and the love others gave me but I just could not express it.

Being recognized for doing well hardly ever happened throughout my childhood. My achievements have been undermined and were non-existent. My mom would not be happy for me. For example, I recall when I played the flute extremely well and all she questioned was why I was watching the music director as if I was infatuated with him. Unknowingly, men weren't even my cup of tea. The entire band watched him because he would direct us to place the flute up or down to play it. If the cues were missed, the band would not move uniformly. Another occurrence is when the monthly awards ceremony rolled around, I would be awarded perfect attendance, honor roll and I even won an art contest but no one was there in the audience to celebrate me or cheer me on. Out of necessity, everyone was working or doing their own thing. When someone was there, there were criticisms more than cheering me on. Still I wanted someone there to see me, to see the real me. I wanted to have someone be proud of me like all the other kids.

At work one day, I had been working diligently and I learned the ins and outs of my work. The manager came one day and played a stupid joke on me. She began talking to me with appreciation and I thought it was real but she was just joking with me and didn't give me anything. I felt so disappointed and stupid. At the start I was thinking aw and began to feel my eyes watering thinking I was actually being appreciated. Instead it was a joke. I stepped away to have a moment to myself and returned back when I was ready. I was crushed to feel vulnerable again only to be seen as the target of a cruel joke.

Trailblazer Void

In my Latino culture, it's rude to not accept what people give us. Commonly people say if you get lemons, make lemonade or something like that when things don't go your way. In a way, it is saying to accept what is and agree with anything & everything without considering your own wants or needs. However, there are times when accepting what others want for you is right out not in alignment with your life. I say, why do I need to accept what you give me? I don't want the lemons nor do I want to make lemonade. Take it back please. Or simply politely stated, no, thank you.

We have been conditioned to accept our current situation, our current circumstances and our current environment. We are taught to be kind. Be a person who accepts gifts that we didn't ask for that we will never use and that will undoubtedly make for more waste in our homes. Yet for many years I just took what was given to me because I was brainwashed to believe I had to.

We aren't taught to say, my preference is this or that. I was taught to be grateful for what we had because what I had was not easy to obtain. Asking for what I wanted was a language that didn't exist until it did. Prior to understanding this, I accepted the titles, the labels, the names, the personal path and career journey others before me had until I learned I don't need to follow the same road traveled as those before me. My trajectory is completely different so why should I take the same staircase to the same floor someone else rose to? Why can't I teach others where my path can lead to? Why can't I be the person who is no longer following the crowd? I've done the same as those before but better and I've taken my role beyond what it has seen before. My role is on a different journey. Therefore it should end differently too.

When you pave your own way, you sacrifice winning for the sake of others. Because you create winning for others sometimes you can't also give it to yourself but there are still opportunities to take respect in other ways. I say take purposely because this has to be intentional. The world, or the mindset of abundance, will find a way to reward you. It will most certainly look different than it ever has before and it will come. You will need to know how to ask for it and what to call it when the time comes because others won't know what you're ready for as well as what it is called because you're initiating this new journey.

Trail your own path for the sake of transforming your own journey, not mapping out the same journey as others but your very own journey. A journey that requires you to dig deep into your own instinct and maybe even I.N.K. in your own destiny. Be a gate-breaker that can rewrite the path forward and with the right strategy you can help others along too. Remember that showing our emotions doesn't make us weak, they make us human and is this not what we are here on earth to experience? To truly feel? To truly be free? Never doubt that I.N.K. and Instinct can transform you in more ways than you know.

Broken Mirrors to Polished Pearls: Your Blueprint for Triumph

There are no accidents in this life. Every moment, every wound, every victory, they're all connected in a tapestry that only makes sense when you step back far enough to see the pattern.

I started this journey with you in the red brick buildings of Passaic, a little Mexican girl with big eyes and bigger dreams, hungry in more ways than one. Now we stand here together at the summit, not because the mountains moved, but because we climbed them, one painful, deliberate step after another.

Remember the fractured foundations? The one-bedroom apartment where dreams seemed impossible and chaos reigned? That same girl who cooked macaroni to survive now sits in corporate boardrooms making decisions that impact thousands. The child who shared sweaters with her brother now mentors others on building their professional brand from negative zero to executive suite, not by magic, but by method.

Our Story Isn't Meant to be a Fairytale It's Meant to be a Blueprint

When my friend's body fell in that pool hall, something in me died too. The belief that life would never be fair or easy, but something else was born in that moment: the fierce determination that if I survived, it would be for a reason. The fact that you're reading these words means that determination wasn't misplaced. My tattoos tell the story of my wounds; my pearls showcase what those wounds became with time and intention.

Think of all we've overcome together. The weight of raising three children from the young age of 21. The invisibility of being "the Mexican girl" in rooms where power wasn't designed to include me. The heartache of parents who couldn't, or wouldn't, see me. Each of these moments could have been an ending. Instead, I transformed them into beginnings.

This is Where Your Journey and Mine Intersect

I've laid out the tools for you throughout these pages. I've shown you how Instinct guided me through dangerous neighborhoods and corporate hierarchies alike. I've revealed how Navigation helped me chart paths where none existed before. I've demonstrated how a Killer Mindset transforms limitations into launching pads. The I.N.K. framework isn't just my story, it's your roadmap.

And P.E.A.R.L.S.? That's your strategy for winning on your own terms:

Positioning yourself where opportunity can find you. **Executing** with such consistency that your reputation precedes you. **Adapting** to setbacks without abandoning your destination. **Resilience** that turns trauma into your teacher. **Leveraging** every relationship to multiply your impact. **Sovereignty** that lets you operate from your center of power.

My grandmother once told me, "You're going to be okay. You're not the first and you won't be the last." Her kitchen, that small, aromatic space where I became her right hand after her injury, was the first place I understood that brokenness can be healed through connection. When she couldn't do everything herself, we did it together, and somehow it became more than either of us could have created alone.

That's the Secret I Want to Leave With You

Your Jackie, that inner critic with the voice of all your doubts and insecurities, will always try to convince you that you're not enough. She'll remind of every mistake, every rejection, every moment you felt small. But your Sunny is there too, whispering the truth: that you were made for more than surviving. You were made for thriving.

I know what it's like to feel invisible. To be the one who makes others uncomfortable because you challenge the status quo. To switch between languages and worlds, never quite belonging in either. To be "la chismosa" too loud, too much, too different. But I also know what it's like to transform that difference into your superpower.

This is my hand reaching back to pull you forward. This is my voice saying what I needed to hear all those years ago: You belong here. Your differences are your strengths. Your struggles are preparing you for something greater.

I never had a roadmap. I carved my path with the tools of necessity and determination. I worked in the emergency lane because sometimes that's the only way to reach your destination when the main road isn't built for people like us. I learned to read rooms before I entered them because my survival depended on it. I built networks because I understood early that no one rises alone.

Now you have what I didn't: a guide who has walked this path before you.

The world will tell you to assimilate, to make yourself smaller, to accept the lemons and make lemonade. Bring your own recipe instead. To stand in your sovereignty. To recognize that the game has rules, but exceptional players rewrite them.

As I look back on the journey from those red brick buildings to executive leadership, from invisibility to influence, I realize that every chapter was necessary.

Even the painful ones, especially the painful ones, shaped me into who I am today. The little girl who lost her friend, the teenager who became a mother too soon, the professional who created roles where none existed, they're all me. They're all part of the story.

And What a Story It Is

I want you to remember that your past doesn't determine your future, it prepares you for it. Your traumas aren't your destiny, they're your training ground. Your differences aren't your weakness, they're your edge.

Like the pearls I've collected over decades, you too are being formed by pressure and persistence. The irritants that once caused you pain are transforming into something luminous and valuable. This process can't be rushed. It happens in its own time, layer by layer, insight by insight. I'm proud of the woman I've become. Not because I'm perfect, I'm gloriously, authentically imperfect, but because I'm powerful in a way that no one can take from me. Not my father from his prison cell. Not my mother with her emotional distance. Not the managers who underestimated me. Not the systems designed to keep me out.

This Power is Mine and the Tools to Claim Your Own Are Now Yours

So what will you do with them? How will you transform your tattoos into pearls? What emergency lanes will you navigate to reach destinations others said were impossible? Who will you become when you stop asking for permission to exist in spaces where your voice matters?

These questions aren't rhetorical. They're invitations to step into your own sovereignty, to chart your own course, to build your own power networks. To recognize that the game doesn't have to be played according to rules that weren't written for you. You can rewrite them. I did.

I.N.K. Framework

Instinct: Trust your authentic reactions to recognition and praise, even when they feel uncomfortable. Your body's response whether it's "resting bitch face" or teary eyes contains wisdom about your past experiences and current boundaries. Learn to distinguish between genuine discomfort with praise versus conditioned responses from childhood experiences.

Navigation: Create your own professional path when established routes don't align with your unique journey. Politely decline opportunities or recognition that don't serve your authentic goals, using "No, thank you" as a complete sentence. Identify mentors who can help you understand the terrain ahead when you're trailblazing a new direction.

Killer Mindset: Transform from accepting what others give you to intentionally designing what you want to receive. Recognize when you're paving new ground and develop language to ask for appropriate acknowledgment. Understand that as a trailblazer, rewards may look different than traditional recognition, so be prepared to define and claim them in new ways.

P.E.A.R.L.S. Strategy

The journey from robotically accepting unwanted recognition to intentionally defining one's own path demonstrates the essence of the P.E.A.R.L.S. strategy. Position yourself authentically rather than conforming to cultural expectations about accepting praise or following predetermined career paths. Execute by setting clear boundaries and articulating what you truly want instead of what others assume you need. Adapt by developing new language and processes for self-advocacy when traditional systems don't recognize your contributions. Build resilience by acknowledging how past experiences shaped your discomfort with recognition while developing healthier responses to praise. Leverage your unique perspective as a trailblazer to create new opportunities not just for yourself but for others who will follow. Ultimately, claim sovereignty by defining success on your own terms, rejecting the "make lemonade" mentality, and intentionally charting a path that honors your authentic self rather than accepting what others believe you should want.

P.E.A.R.L.S. - THE STRATEGY THAT ELEVATES YOU

How to Win the Game on Your Own Terms

The journey from brokenness to brilliance isn't direct. There's no perfect path, no single staircase that leads to the top. My life has been a collection of broken mirrors, emergency lanes, and fearful steps forward. Yet here I stand, an executive, an author, a voice for others who feel they don't belong in spaces of power.

How did I navigate this path? Through a strategy I've refined with every setback, every triumph, every boundary crossed. I call it P.E.A.R.L.S. because like the precious gem formed through pressure and persistence, your own power develops the same way.

P – POSITIONING: Build Your Brand

I learned early that visibility precedes opportunity. At the volleyball court, in the Hispanic Society, in every meeting room, I made sure people saw me before I spoke. I didn't wait to be called on; I claimed my space.

Positioning isn't just about being seen; it's about being remembered. It's about crafting a reputation so distinct that when opportunities arise, your name surfaces naturally. When I wanted a Senior Advisor role that didn't exist, I positioned myself as the obvious solution to a problem they hadn't fully articulated yet.

Start by asking: What unique perspective do I bring? What do I want to be known for? Then place yourself directly in the conversations that matter. Sit at the table, not against the wall. Speak early in meetings, not just when called upon. Make them see you first.

E – EXECUTION: Show Up and Deliver

Ideas without execution are just daydreams. I didn't just join employee resource groups, I transformed them and later created one. I didn't just manage projects, I exceeded their scope. When working with my grandmother after her injury, I didn't just help, I added my own flair.

Excellence isn't accidental; it's intentional. It's about promising only what you can deliver, then delivering more than you promised. I watched so many talented people fade into the background because they couldn't translate potential into performance.

The secret? Consistency. I showed up every day at the volleyball court, even after fights on my way home. I answered every customer service call with the same energy, regardless of what was happening in my personal life. People learned they could count on me, and that reliability became my superpower.

A – ADAPTABILITY: Know When to Pivot

Life rarely follows our perfect plans. My path to college was interrupted by motherhood. My relationships were complicated by trauma.

127

What separates those who thrive from those who survive is adaptability, the willingness to change direction without abandoning your destination. When I was offered two positions, supervising and entry-level, I chose the lower one because I saw the bigger picture.

Adaptability isn't weakness; it's strategic flexibility. It's understanding that sometimes the direct path isn't the smartest one. Sometimes you need to step back to leap forward. My willingness to craft roles that didn't exist, to volunteer for projects nobody wanted, to build skills nobody expected, these pivots made all the difference. To help those in need that seemed like misfits. To the fact that people say I built my own Empire!

R – RESILIENCE & REWARD: Bounce Back Stronger & Celebrate Your Wins

My mother never showed up to my performances. My father created a second family while still married. I have raised three children since the age of 21. I could have let these experiences define my limits rather than fuel my determination.

Resilience isn't about ignoring pain; it's about using it as your teacher. Every time I was passed over for promotion, every time someone questioned my abilities, every time I faced rejection I asked, "What can I learn here?"

But resilience without reward is just endurance. We must celebrate our victories, no matter how small. When I completed my degree after years of trying, I didn't just mark it off my list, I honored the journey. When I reached the executive level, I didn't pretend it was expected; I acknowledged it was extraordinary.

The rewards aren't just external. The greatest reward is becoming someone who can face any challenge without flinching, someone who knows their worth isn't determined by others' validation.

L – LEVERAGE: Maximize Every Connection

No one rises alone. I've leveraged mentors, sponsors, colleagues, and even adversaries to propel my journey forward. As Woodrow Wilson said, "I not only use the brains I have but all I can borrow."

Leverage isn't manipulation; it's multiplication. It's recognizing that relationships are investments that compound over time. When I partnered with others on projects, we both reached heights neither could achieve alone. When I learned from others' expertise, it accelerated my growth beyond what solo effort could accomplish.

My grandmother showed me the power of leverage when she told me, "Look, by myself I have a little bit and your grandfather has a little bit, but when we combine it together, look at what we have managed to do." This principle applies everywhere, from resources to relationships to reputation.

S – SOVEREIGNTY: Build Your Own Power

Ultimately, P.E.A.R.L.S. leads to sovereignty, the state of operating from your own center of power rather than constantly reacting to external forces. I no longer need validation from parents who couldn't give it. I don't require permission to create the role I envision. I'm not waiting for invitations to spaces where my voice matters.

Sovereignty means owning your narrative. It means defining success on your terms. It means understanding that power isn't given, it's claimed and then shared.

This doesn't mean isolation. Quite the opposite. My greatest influence emerged when I stopped trying to fit into existing structures and started building my own. When I created roles, structures, frameworks and improvements where none existed. When I published my story despite its imperfections. When I mentored others because I remembered how it felt to navigate without a map, without support. Even when I passed the baton, walking away from what we built together, when they thought they weren't ready, were all part of getting them ready to build their own.

The Polished Strategy That Makes You Unstoppable

P.E.A.R.L.S. isn't a quick fix or a surface-level approach. It's about playing chess, not checkers or in my case, playing pool, leveraging every move, relationship, and lesson to carve out your space without losing your edge.

It's recognizing that the game has rules, but the truly exceptional players rewrite them. It's understanding that your greatest disadvantages, my chaotic childhood, my early motherhood, my outsider status can become your greatest advantages when properly channeled.

I stand before you now not as someone who conquered the world without struggle, but as living proof that brokenness and brilliance can coexist. That the emergency lane sometimes gets you there faster.

My I.N.K. framework: Instinct, Navigation, & a Killer Mindset provided the foundation. P.E.A.R.L.S. built the structure. And now, it's your turn to create the masterpiece. **Remember:** *You don't have to be perfect to be powerful. You just have to be strategically, authentically, unapologetically you.* And that, my friends, is how we win the game on our own terms.

THE SECRET'S OUT!

The Journey Toward Self-Acceptance and Healing

The secret has finally emerged from the shadows; my life's journey wasn't meant to stay hidden in the corners of my past. Throughout these pages, I've shared glimpses of my path from those red brick buildings to executive leadership, from invisibility to influence. What began as a necessity for survival has transformed into wisdom I can now share with the world.

Looking back on this journey, I recognize a profound truth: the path to self-acceptance is nonlinear. It's a constantly evolving relationship with yourself, a daily practice of showing up authentically despite every instinct to retreat back into invisibility. For decades, I perfected the art of being unseen, a skill that protected me but also confined me. The patterns established in childhood became the foundation upon which I built walls rather than bridges, creating a fortress around my heart that kept pain out but also prevented connection from getting in.

The irony wasn't lost on me that while others perceived me as confident and outspoken "la chismosa" with the voice that could project across distances, internally I remained that vulnerable child, hypervigilant and waiting for the next disappointment. This dissonance between my external presentation and internal reality created its own kind of exhaustion. I became an expert at managing perceptions while keeping my true self hidden, a survival strategy that served me well in chaotic environments but ultimately limited my capacity to experience genuine joy and connection.

When I finally chose to step into the light, to claim space not just for myself but for others who shared my experience, something extraordinary happened. The invisibility that once felt like my prison became my perspective, a unique vantage point that allowed me to see systems, organizations, and relationships differently than those who had always belonged. I began to recognize patterns in corporate structures that others couldn't see, identify inefficiencies in processes that others had normalized, and build connections across silos that others perceived as impenetrable.

The day I realized my differences were actually my strengths marked the beginning of true healing. My bilingual mind didn't make me less intelligent; it gave me cognitive flexibility that others lacked. My experiences navigating poverty didn't make me deficient; they gave me resourcefulness that others never developed. My journey as a young mother didn't limit my potential; it accelerated my leadership development in ways traditional paths never could. The very experiences that had caused me shame became the foundation of my unique value proposition.

This revelation didn't happen overnight. It came through years of intentional work, therapy, coaching, and surrounding myself with people who saw me clearly when I couldn't yet see myself. It came from learning to distinguish between the voices of limitation and the voices of possibility. It came through recognizing that the inner critic I called "Jackie," that voice questioning whether I belonged, whether I deserved success, wasn't actually me.

My healing journey required me to examine every relationship, every belief, every pattern I had accepted as truth. I had to confront generational traumas not to dwell in them, but to ensure they ended with me. I had to acknowledge the ways I had participated in my own invisibility, the moments when staying small felt safer than risking rejection. I had to recognize how I had unconsciously recreated familiar patterns of chaos and struggle because they felt like home, even when they no longer served my growth.

Most importantly, I had to forgive not just others, but myself. Forgive myself for the times I dismissed my own voice. Forgive myself for believing I had to choose between authenticity and acceptance. Forgive myself for years spent seeking validation from people incapable of providing it. Forgive myself for the moments when survival took precedence over thriving, when I chose safety over growth because that was what I needed at the time.

The profound lesson in my healing journey wasn't about becoming someone new but about uncovering who I had always been beneath layers of protection and adaptation. The leadership voice that now commands executive rooms was always there; it just needed permission to emerge. The strategic thinking that transformed organizations was always there; it just needed to be applied beyond survival. The capacity for genuine connection that enriches my relationships today was always there; it just needed to feel safe enough to express itself.

My journey toward self-acceptance required me to rewrite the story I told about myself. Instead of viewing my past through the lens of deficiency, I began to see how every challenge had equipped me with unique capabilities:

I.N.K. Framework

Instinct: Years of navigating potentially dangerous situations gave me an unmatched ability to read people and environments. What began as a survival mechanism became an executive superpower, sensing undercurrents in meetings, identifying genuine allies, and recognizing opportunities others missed. That hypervigilance that once exhausted me became refined intuition that now guides me through complex professional landscapes.

Think about the moments in your own life when you've sensed something before you could articulate it. That feeling in your gut telling you when something isn't right, when someone isn't being truthful, when an opportunity is worth pursuing despite conventional wisdom. That instinct isn't random, it's pattern recognition operating at a level beyond conscious thought, drawing on every experience you've ever had. Instead of dismissing these feelings as irrational, I learned to honor them as valuable data points.

Navigation: Finding paths where none existed wasn't just how I survived childhood it became how

I transformed organizations. Creating roles that didn't previously exist, building bridges between siloed departments, and developing programs that met needs no one had formally acknowledged all stemmed from this foundational skill. My ability to adapt to changing circumstances, to pivot when necessary without losing sight of the destination, became the cornerstone of my professional success.

Consider how you've navigated your own challenging terrains, the times when the conventional path wasn't available to you, when you had to create alternatives, when you discovered shortcuts others hadn't considered. These navigation skills develop most powerfully in those who cannot take the default route, who must constantly reassess and recalibrate. What if these weren't detours from your path but actually the path itself – the unique journey that only you could travel?

Killer Mindset: The determination that helped me break cycles of poverty, abuse, and limitation became the same force that propelled me through corporate hierarchies. The unwavering belief that there's always another way, another approach, another solution continues to define my leadership today. This isn't about toxic positivity or denying reality, it's about refusing to accept current limitations as permanent boundaries.

Reflect on the moments when you've persisted despite overwhelming odds, when you've found reserves of strength you didn't know you possessed, when you've maintained focus on your destination even when the path seemed impossible. This killer mindset isn't about aggression, it's about unstoppable determination, about the refusal to be defined by others' expectations or limitations.

These three elements, Instinct, Navigation, and Killer Mindset, formed my personal I.N.K. framework, the foundation upon which I built everything else. But survival alone wasn't enough. I wanted to thrive, to create something lasting, to transform not just my own story but the narrative for others who would follow.

That's where my P.E.A.R.L.S. strategy emerged:

P.E.A.R.L.S. Strategy

Positioning: I learned to place myself where opportunity could find me, building a distinctive professional brand that made me memorable and indispensable. This wasn't about self-promotion in the traditional sense, but about strategic visibility ensuring that my unique contributions were recognized and valued. I stopped waiting to be discovered and started deliberately showcasing my strengths.

In your own career, consider: Are you positioned where your unique talents can shine? Have you created a professional narrative that highlights your distinctive perspective? Are you in environments where your contributions will be recognized and rewarded? Positioning isn't about pretending to be something you're not, it's about ensuring that your authentic gifts are visible to those who need them most.

Execution: I delivered consistently above expectations, creating a reputation for excellence that opened doors even when formal credentials couldn't. My commitment to flawless implementation meant that people learned they could count on me not just for big ideas but for reliable results. This consistency became my signature in environments where promises often went unfulfilled.

Consider your own execution standards: Do you consistently deliver on commitments? Have you built a reputation for reliability that precedes you? Do people know that when you take on a responsibility, it will be handled with excellence? Excellence in execution creates a foundation of trust that no credential can replace.

Adaptability: I remained flexible about methods while staying committed to destinations, pivoting when necessary without abandoning my ultimate goals. This willingness to adjust course in response to changing circumstances, unexpected obstacles, or new information became particularly valuable in rapidly transforming industries and organizations.

Reflect on your own adaptability: How quickly do you adjust to changing circumstances? Can you let go of attachment to specific methods when they no longer serve your goals? Do you distinguish between core commitments that must remain stable and tactical approaches that can evolve? Adaptability isn't about abandoning your principles; it's about finding multiple paths to honor them.

Resilience: I developed the capacity to bounce back stronger from setbacks, viewing challenges as temporary and extracting wisdom from every difficult experience. This wasn't about denying pain or disappointment, but about refusing to let these moments define my future possibilities. I learned to celebrate small wins along the way, creating a reservoir of positive experiences to draw upon during challenging times.

In your own journey, consider: How quickly do you recover from disappointments? Have you developed practices that help you maintain perspective during difficult times? Do you consistently extract learning from challenges rather than merely enduring them? Resilience isn't innate, it's cultivated through intentional practices and supportive relationships.

Leverage: I maximized every relationship and connection, creating networks of mutual support that accelerated growth for everyone involved. I recognized early that advancement never happens in isolation; we rise by lifting others, by creating reciprocal relationships where everyone benefits from shared success. This approach transformed competitive environments into collaborative ones, where collective wisdom produced better outcomes than individual brilliance.

Think about your own approach to relationships: Do you build connections based on mutual benefit rather than transactional advantage? Have you created networks that provide support during challenges and amplification during successes? Do you actively seek opportunities to connect others who might benefit from knowing each other? Leverage isn't about using people, it's about creating ecosystems where everyone thrives.

Sovereignty: I claimed authority over my own narrative and professional path, creating roles that showcased my unique talents rather than forcing myself into predetermined boxes. This internal locus of control meant that I stopped waiting for permission to lead, to innovate, to transform. I recognized that power isn't granted, it's claimed and then shared.

Consider your own sovereignty: Have you taken ownership of your professional narrative? Do you create opportunities rather than waiting for them to be offered? Have you defined success on your own terms rather than accepting external definitions? Sovereignty isn't about isolation; it's about interdependence from a place of personal power.

This isn't just my professional strategy, it's become my life philosophy. The same approach that transformed my career has also healed my relationships with myself, my children, my partner, and even my past. The principles that guided me through corporate hierarchies have proven equally valuable in personal growth, parenting, and community leadership.

The final element of my healing journey has been the willingness to be open about my imperfections. For someone who spent decades trying to be flawless to avoid criticism or rejection, choosing vulnerability has been revolutionary. Sharing my story, not the sanitized version but the messy, complicated truth, represented my ultimate act of self-acceptance.

This vulnerability doesn't mean abandoning boundaries or exposing wounds before they've healed. It means accepting that our humanity, including our struggles, our failures, and our uncertainties, is not a liability but a point of connection. It means recognizing that the very experiences I once tried desperately to hide are precisely what allow me to connect authentically with others on similar journeys.

I recognize now that my voice matters precisely because of where it comes from. My perspective holds value specifically because it emerged from experiences that many would rather not acknowledge. My leadership resonates because it comes from someone who understands both struggle and triumph intimately. The credibility I've earned comes not in spite of my unconventional path, but because of it.

This realization has transformed how I show up in every context — in boardrooms and living rooms, in professional settings and personal relationships. I no longer exhaust myself trying to be someone else's version of perfect. I bring my whole self to every interaction, knowing that my authenticity is my greatest asset. I speak my truth not with apology but with the confidence that comes from knowing its value.

The freedom that comes with this authenticity cannot be overstated. When you're no longer investing energy in maintaining an image or hiding parts of yourself, that energy becomes available for creativity, connection, and contribution. When you stop worrying about being found out as an impostor, you can focus entirely on the work you're here to do. When you embrace all aspects of your story, including the painful chapters, they lose their power to control you.

The secret's out and it's this: You don't have to hide the parts of yourself that don't fit conventional expectations. Those very elements are likely your most significant sources of wisdom and strength. You don't have to choose between authenticity and achievement. Your most genuine self is actually your most powerful professional asset. You don't have to overcome your past you can transform it into the foundation of your unique contribution.

My life's work has become creating spaces where others can make this same discovery, where they can transform their own wounds into wisdom, their challenges into competitive advantages. The little girl from those red brick buildings, who once felt invisible, now stands in boardrooms, ensuring others are seen. The teenager who faced loss and limitation now creates pathways of possibility for the next generation. The young mother who struggled to balance responsibilities now mentors others navigating similar terrains.

This journey toward self-acceptance and healing isn't finished; it's ongoing, evolving, and deepening. Each new level of success brings its own challenges, each new relationship tests old patterns, and each new opportunity invites me to either retreat into familiar limitations or expand into new possibilities. The difference now is that I face these moments with awareness rather than automaticity, with choice rather than compulsion.

I've learned that healing doesn't mean erasing the past, it means integrating it into a larger story where pain becomes purposeful. It doesn't mean forgetting trauma, it means transforming it into insight. It doesn't mean pretending the hard times never happened, it means honoring how they shaped you without allowing them to control you.

The secret is no longer a secret. The power that lived in me all along has been released, and I invite you to unleash yours as well. The world doesn't need more people who fit perfectly into systems designed without them in mind. It requires more people who will bring their full, messy, brilliant authenticity to transform those systems. It needs your unique voice, shaped by every experience you've ever had. It needs your distinctive perspective, informed by challenges others haven't faced.

Your tattoos tell the story of where you've been. Your pearls showcase what those experiences have become with time and intention. Both are equally valuable parts of your leadership narrative. Both deserve to be honored, integrated, and expressed.

The journey from invisibility to influence isn't about leaving your past behind; it's about bringing it forward with purpose. It's about transforming personal pain into collective healing, individual challenges into systemic solutions. It's about recognizing that the very experiences that once seemed to disqualify you from leadership may be your greatest qualifications.

The secret's out. And now, it's your turn to claim it.

A LETTER I WROTE TO MYSELF 2 YEARS AGO!

Miriam June 23, 2023 Written during my Hudson Coaching Process

Dear Miriam,

As you indulge in your abilities, capabilities, and all that is yet to come, think of the power that is within you that has transcended you beyond. Feeling alive, well, and ready for your day is what you've dreamed of! Being and doing are what you do best. There really is no other like you, and live your life out loud and in color! Doing for you will allow you to be the best version of yourself to live a long, HAPPY life. Being HAPPY is where your joy, energy, and power come from! Let the distractions fade into the clouds and dissipate.

Your body has come a long way and will continue to serve you.

Your future clients will thank you for all you've been able to give, and the opportunity you make happen will be enjoyed by many.

As you go into your next chapter, know that everything will be okay and you'll continue to find the way.

Your book was the start to the greatness within you that has been there all along.

Remember that invisibility is no longer serving you. The calling is to SHOW UP.

With love,

Miriam Simon

FINAL HEARTFELT MESSAGE

That's my final message to you. Show up not as who they expect you to be, but as who you truly are. Bring your full, unapologetic, strategically brilliant self to every table, every conversation, every opportunity. Your journey from shadow to stardom won't look like mine, but the principles that guide it will be the same.

Trust your instinct. Navigate with intention. Maintain a killer mindset.

Position yourself strategically. Execute with excellence. Adapt when necessary. Build resilience. Leverage every connection. Claim your sovereignty.

Your brokenness was never meant to break you permanently. It was meant to break you open – to reveal the strength, wisdom, and power that were there all along, waiting for the moment when you'd be ready to claim them.

That moment is now.

From red bricks to black ink, from scarcity to abundance, from invisibility to influence, this is more than my story. It's the blueprint for yours.

Go make it extraordinary.

With boundless faith in you, Miriam

READY TO APPLY THE I.N.K. FRAMEWORK

and P.E.A.R.L.S. Strategy for Your Unique Challenges?

As a Certified Hudson Professional Development Coach, I guide professionals ready to break through their limitations and claim their power. Whether you're:

✓ Navigating corporate environments where you feel invisible
✓ Building your confidence and strategic presence
✓ Creating your own path where traditional routes have failed you
✓ Transforming personal struggles into professional strengths

Your story isn't finished. Let's write your next chapter together.

Visit www.MiriamSimon.online to schedule a complimentary strategy session where we'll identify your immediate opportunities for transformation.

The emergency lane is waiting. Are you ready to drive?

ABOUT THE AUTHOR

Miriam Simon is a trailblazing leadership coach, author, and speaker who blends over 25 years of corporate leadership with deep personal insight to guide others toward success. As the author of her latest leadership book "Tattoos & Pearls", she marries street-smart resilience with corporate strategy, showing the world how to thrive authentically in high-pressure environments. A Certified Hudson Coach, Forbes Coaches Council Member, and Corporate Achiever Award recipient, Miriam's expertise spans Human Resources, leadership development, and employee relations.

Throughout her career, Miriam has been a pivotal force in strategic initiatives and workforce optimization, using her profound knowledge to drive meaningful change. Her transformative leadership style, honed through extensive work with employee resource groups, culminated in a senior advisor/co-Sponsor role, further establishing her as a trusted leader in corporate spaces.

But it's Miriam's mission that sets her apart. She's dedicated to supporting one million marginalized voices in reaching leadership roles in corporate environments, believing in the power of authenticity and representation at the highest levels. Her coaching is grounded in her own experiences of overcoming adversity both as a strong Latina leader and a leading voice in the LGBTQ+ community, along with building an impactful career while staying true to her values. She does this by engaging her audience in her podcast "Latina Mic-Drop," currently on all major music platforms.

Clients who work with Miriam unlock their full potential, combining their authentic selves with the tools to excel in the corporate world. She offers a rare combination of empathy, strategic insight, and a relentless drive to help others succeed. Whether you're navigating executive leadership or building a future from scratch, Miriam empowers you to own your story, take up space, and lead with confidence.

Miriam is CEO and Founder of Mi Sí Coaching and Consulting LLC and is redefining leadership with her podcast: Latina Mic Drop.

www.miriamsimon.online

BONUS CONTENT

FREE Tattoos & Pearls 5-Step Quick Start Guide
This bold, no-BS guide is your first move toward owning your power. In five simple yet impactful steps, you'll begin aligning your lived experiences with leadership strategy so you can stop shrinking and start showing up fully. Whether you're stepping into a new role or reclaiming your voice, this guide is your launchpad.

Free Exclusive 90-Minute Live Pearls of Wisdom Webinar with Me
Join me for a no-fluff, high-impact session where we'll break down the key strategies from the book and talk real talk about how to activate your leadership power, heal through action, and take up space in any room you walk into.

The Tattoos & Pearls Companion Workbook
A guided space to reflect, take notes, and apply the insights in your own voice and power. This isn't just a workbook, it's your strategy lab, your truth table, your mirror.

152

www.ingramcontent.com/pod-product-compliance
Lightning Source LLC
Chambersburg PA
CBHW071403120626
46546CB00002B/789